BT 8112

I0699249

GAME **PLAN**
FOR LIFE

GAME PLAN
FOR LIFE

CHALK TALKS

JOE GIBBS

ZONDERVAN®

ZONDERVAN.com/
AUTHORTRACKER
follow your favorite authors

ZONDERVAN

Game Plan for Life: Chalk Talks
Copyright © 2012 by Joe Gibbs

This title is also available as a Zondervan ebook.
Visit www.zondervan.com/ebooks.

This title is also available in a Zondervan audio edition.
Visit www.zondervan.fm.

Requests for information should be addressed to:

Zondervan, *Grand Rapids, Michigan 49530*

Library of Congress Cataloging-in-Publication Data

Gibbs, Joe, 1940-
    Game plan for life : chalk talks / Joe Gibbs.
       p.   cm.
    ISBN 978-0-310-33037-0
    1. Christian men – Religious life. 2. Success – Religious aspects –
Christianity. 3. Chalk-talks. I. Title.
BV4528.2.G525 2012
248.8'42 – dc23   2012015779

Cover design: James Hall
Cover photo: Shutterstock / iStockphoto®
Interior design: Kathy Ristow, CouGrr Graphics
Interior illustration: iStockphoto®
Photo insert design: Sarah Johnson
Photo insert images: Joe Gibbs, Autostock for Joe Gibbs Racing, Bryan Cook/Joe
Gibbs Racing, iStockphoto®

Printed in the United States of America

12 13 14 15 16 17 18 19 /DCI/ 19 18 17 16 15 14 13 12 11 10 9 8 7 6 5 4 3 2 1

CONTENTS

TIME LINE OF JOE GIBBS

November 25, 1940	Born in Mocksville, North Carolina
1955	Relocated to southern California with family
1959	Graduated Santa Fe High School, Santa Fe, California
1959 – 1963	Attended Cerritos Junior College and San Diego State University (SDSU)
1964 – 1966	Graduated from SDSU and earned a master's degree in 1966
	Started coaching career under Don Coryell as a graduate assistant
January 29, 1966	Married Pat
1967 – 1968	Offensive line coach for Florida State University
1969 – 1970	Coached under John McKay at Southern California (USC)
February 21, 1969	First son, J.D. Gibbs, was born
1971 – 1972	Coached under Frank Broyles at University of Arkansas
December 9, 1972	Second son, Coy Gibbs, was born
1973 – 1977	Rejoined Coryell as running backs coach for St. Louis Cardinals
1978	Offensive coordinator under John McKay for Tampa Bay Buccaneers
1979 – 1980	Rejoined Coryell once again as offensive coordinator for the San Diego Chargers

1981	Named head coach of Washington Redskins
January 1983	Redskins win Super Bowl XVII
January 1988	Redskins win Super Bowl XXII
1991	Announced the formation of Joe Gibbs Racing (JGR)
1992	Redskins win Super Bowl XXVI
1993	JGR wins first-ever NASCAR race with the 1993 running of the Daytona 500
March 1993	Gibbs retires as head coach of the Washington Redskins after twelve seasons
October 1997	Son, J.D. Gibbs, named president of JGR
2000	JGR wins its first NASCAR Cup championship, with driver Bobby LaBonte
2002	JGR wins its second NASCAR Cup championship, with driver Tony Stewart
January 2004	Gibbs returns as head coach of the Washington Redskins
2005	JGR wins its third NASCAR Cup championship, with driver Tony Stewart
January 2008	JGR Motocross (JGRMX) founded by son, Coy Gibbs, runs first race
January 2008	Gibbs resigns as head coach of Washington Redskins
2008	JGR wins NASCAR Nationwide Series Owner's Championship
August 2009	*Game Plan for Life,* Coach Gibbs' third book, becomes *NY Times* bestseller
2009	JGR wins NASCAR Nationwide Series Driver's and Owner's Championship
2010	JGR wins NASCAR Nationwide Series Championship

FROM THE COACH

What does it mean to win? How do you define success? My entire adult life has involved competition in two professional sports with over 100 million fans between them. As the head coach of the Washington Redskins, we won three Super Bowls and four NFC championships. As the owner of Joe Gibbs Racing, we've won three NASCAR Cup championships and over 175 races so far. Along the way I've learned a lot about what it takes to win. But, you know what? I also know something about losing.

Standing on the sideline in front of 91,000 fans at FedEx Field in Washington when a decision I made may have contributed to the Redskins' defeat is tough. Watching one of our cars dominate a 500-mile race only to get taken out by equipment failure is hard to take. In my personal life I haven't always been the perfect husband and dad. To be truthful with you, many of the most important lessons I've learned in my life have come from personal failures and professional losses.

Along the way I've learned the value of setting aside time to connect with the Lord by reading the Bible, praying, and doing a short devotional; this time is one of the most important resources I have to live successfully. My quiet time with the Lord gives me perspective and the strength to get up and move into the day with the assurance that my Heavenly Father cares for me and is interested in helping me find true success — as He defines it.

When it comes right down to it, I'm just your "average Joe" looking for practical solutions to the challenges life throws at me. I believe God gives us the guidance we need in His Word. Maybe you're like me, and if that's the case, my hope is that as you read these devotionals, you'll be encouraged to "trust in the LORD with all your heart and lean not on your own understanding" so that He can "make your paths straight" (Proverbs 3:5 – 6).

WINNING THE GAME OF LIFE

Commit to the LORD whatever you do,
and he will establish your plans.
PROVERBS 16:3

From the time I was a young kid in middle school my hope was to one day become a professional football player — I loved competing against other teams and taking on challenges with my teammates. Later, at San Diego State, it became clear to me that although I was a decent football player, I just didn't have the skill it would take to become a great professional player. I set my sights on coaching instead, starting as a gradu- ate assistant at SDSU under Aztec head coach Don Coryell. Pat and I have never looked back — coaching is one of the things I was created to do.

One thing I love about coaching is that there is no mystery at the end of a game. The scoreboard says it all — when that clock runs out and your sixty minutes are up, the only thing that matters is the final score. Someone wins; someone loses. I was fortunate to win a few Super Bowls as the head coach of the Washington Redskins and to end my football career with a winning record. Along the way I learned a lot from those wins, but I learned a lot from the losses as well. I believe that God used my experience in the NFL to impact the way I look at life.

As a coach, I view life as a game. You and I are the players. When our life on earth is over, there's going to be a scoreboard. Matthew 16:27 puts it like this, "For the Son of Man is going to come in his Father's glory with his angels, and then he will reward each person according to what they have done." If you're like me, you want to be on the winning team when the clock stops. The game of life is the most important game you'll ever play, and whether you win or lose there will be eternal consequences.

How do we make sure we're on the winning team? Well, if we are in a game, we have to have a coach. I believe our head coach in the game of life is God. Does a good coach just put his team on the field and say, "Go get 'em, guys ... Do your best ... I hope you win"? Nope. He wants the best for his players and crafts a specific game plan for them to succeed. I believe that God has given us the perfect game plan, which we can find in His playbook, the Bible.

In my experience, every time I veer away from God's game plan I run into trouble, even disaster. On the other hand, when I'm careful to trust Him and follow His playbook, I find success — maybe not in terms of wins and losses, but in the sense of being at peace knowing that the outcome is in the hands of God who loves me deeply and always wants the best for me. In Romans 8:28 we read, "And we know that in all things God works for the good of those who love him, who have been called according to his purpose."

I've been coaching and leading a long time now and have seen many people promoting countless game plans. Some promise to make you rich. Others promise to help you "maximize your potential" or whatever. I can honestly tell you that in my view there is only one game plan I want to execute. It comes to me from a God who loves me so much that He gave His only Son to pay for my sins. His game plan has a perfect playbook, the Bible, which includes everything I need to be successful in life.

How about you? Are you following a game plan for your life? If it's not God's, how is it working for you? Are you ready to follow the one game plan that promises you'll wind up on the winning team when the clock stops?

Dear Father, thank You for giving us a game plan to live our lives by. We all want to be on the winning team when our lives on this earth are over. We want eternal life in heaven with You. Help me to be disciplined to seek You daily. Help me to turn to Your Word for the plays I need to execute to be successful. Amen.

THE PERFECT COACH

As each NFL season comes to a close, a ritual takes place on the first Monday after the last regular-season game. The sports media call it "Black Monday," when general man-

agers and team owners take stock of how well their team did that year — what went right and what went wrong. Then they look at their head coach, evaluating whether or not he is capable of helping the team per-form at a high level next year. A lot of coaching changes take place on Black Monday. The sports media love to cover the firing and hiring — the "coaching carousel" as they sometimes call it. Being an NFL head coach is not for the faint of heart nor for those seeking job security.

Yet although being a head coach is tough, there is no question he is arguably the most influential factor on any team. He sets the direction, and the coaching staff supports his decisions. The players, from the future Hall of Fame veteran to the greenest rookie, look to him for leadership. They need to have confidence in his skills as a leader and coach. They also need to know that he cares about them and that his job is to help them become the best player they can be. No matter how great the player may be, he will not win a game on his own skills alone. He will win the game by playing on a team with talent that is coached and organized for success.

In the game of life, God — our head coach — is the single most important factor in winning. As the great Christian writer A. W. Tozer noted, "What comes into our minds when we think about God is the most important thing about us."[1] Asking Christ to be my Lord and Savior, submitting to God as my head coach, is the most important decision I've ever made, and it has impacted every area of my life — from how I treat my wife and sons to how I spend my money to how I interact with the people with whom I work. Whether you spend your life trying to collect wealth and fame for yourself or loving others and storing up treasures in heaven depends almost entirely upon how you view God.

And yet so many have not made that connection. Frequently someone will say to me, "Joe, if I had proof that God really did exist, I would believe." To answer this I share four commonsense observations I've made. First, I've witnessed profound changes in other people's lives that are just short of miraculous. I've seen guys completely turn their lives around. Second, I believe the complexity of the universe and creation speaks to the existence of God. Third, the Bible itself is amazing; though people have tried to debunk it throughout history, centuries later it is more relevant than ever with a clear, consistent message and more historical evidence authenticating it every year. Last, I talk about the changes that came about in my own life, some of which are documented on other pages in this devotional.

Have you made God your Head Coach yet? When you think of Him, what comes into your mind? Do you realize that He loves you and cares about the struggles you are facing today and that He wants to be in a relationship with you ... to be the Head Coach in your life? From the very first pages of the Bible, we learn that we are created in the image of God (Genesis 1:27). The rest of the Bible is about His unyielding efforts to be in relationship with fallen mankind. He knows our very thoughts (Psalm 139:4). Why wouldn't we want Him to lead us?

> *Heavenly Father, thank You for being the Coach of my life, always wanting what is best for me. Please help me to know You more intimately. Help me learn to turn to You with all of my struggles, disappointments, and failures. Help me also to learn to talk to You through my prayers and praise You in the best of times. Amen.*

WHAT ARE YOUR IDOLS?

As the 2010 Sprint Cup season was coming to a close, I could hardly sleep. The championship would be decided in one last race at Homestead-Miami Speedway. Leading the pack was our driver, Denny Hamlin, winner of eight races — more than any other driver that season. Yet he was only fifteen points ahead, and within striking range was Jimmie Johnson, a four-time NASCAR champion. It was turning out to be one of the closest chases for the  Cup in history. Competition like this was great for television ratings and sports writers, but it was a lot of pressure on our team, knowing what was at stake.

If you're unfamiliar with NASCAR, the Sprint Cup is the top division. Starting with the Daytona 500 in February, we race thirty-six races. All along the way, drivers and teams rack up points awarded for wins, laps led, and a number of other factors. Whoever has the most points at the end of the season is the champion—the best in the sport.

In the nights before the final race, I lay in bed consumed with how much I wanted to win. I'd think about our employees at Joe Gibbs Racing and how much another championship would mean to them. Then there was FedEx, such a great sponsor—having Denny in victory lane would mean so much to that company and its thousands of employees. Our manufacturer, Toyota, would win its first NASCAR Sprint Cup championship. Then there were the title winnings that go to the victor ... these added financial resources could help in so many areas of our race team. I don't know about you, but my mind can just go on and on like this, especially at night when it is quiet.

But during this time, the Lord had another message for me. No matter how busy I get, I try to spend time studying my Bible and praying daily. Exodus 20:5 was the particular verse in the daily devotional I was reading at that time. This verse is the second of the Ten Commandments: we are to have no idols. Idols are anything we put before the Lord, anything we adore other than God. Often idols are things that we think we can't live without. I had to ask myself, "What if we lose this race? Can I live with that?" It was important for us to do everything within our power to win, but I had to leave the outcome to the Lord.

In my video devotional that week on our *Game Plan for Life* website, I asked people to pray for us. I wanted to make sure that we had the right attitude—no matter how the race turned out. I wanted to make sure that we trusted that our loving God would allow whatever outcome was best for us ... even if it was different than what we hoped it to be.

You know what? I'm glad we had folks pray that prayer! We ended up losing the race and the 2010 championship; we finished second. Denny was devastated. Every competitive bone in my body was disappointed. It was tough on our entire organization, our sponsors, and our families. We had come so close. Talk about an emotional letdown!

But the truth is that as hard as that was for us, I knew in my heart — even in the painful moment of that defeat — that my God always gives me the things that are best for me. This is the same God who gave His only Son to die on a cross for my sins. His plan for us is so much better than one we could ever make for ourselves. My experience working through other disappointing results over the years had given me the knowledge that I could trust Him, no matter how bleak the situation appeared.

What are your idols? For me, I can idolize winning. I'm a competitive guy and I don't like to lose. For you it may be something else. Is it the things you own? Is it your social position? Perhaps winning the next golf game? What about money? Or your kid's athletics? The bottom line here is that you and I are not to let anything get between God and us.

Lord, thank You for the clarity of Your Word. Over and over You show us clearly what we need to do and what we need to avoid. Help me be aware of any idols in my life. Help me to renounce them and stay focused on the one true God who made me, loves me, and knows what's best for me. Amen.

THE PERFECT PLAYBOOK

Your word is a lamp for my feet,
a light on my path.
PSALM 119:105

Have you ever played that party game that starts with a phrase whispered from person to person until the last individual repeats out loud what he was told? Most of the time

it's unrecognizable from the original statement and everyone has a good laugh. It is amazing how easy it is for us to miscommunicate with each other.

Early in my NFL career I had the distinct displeasure of experiencing a similar failure to communicate. At the time I was the offensive coordinator for John McKay at Tampa Bay. John had always called the plays for his offense, but when I joined his coaching staff he was willing to turn play calling over to me. This was before we had electronic communications between the sideline and the quarterback, so we devised a system of hand signals to relay the plays.

Our play-calling system got off to a good start but the season didn't; we lost our first two games. Coach McKay pulled me aside in practice one day. "Joe, I'm not comfortable with these hand signals," he said. "I want you to tell a player on the sideline what play you want; he can run in and tell Doug Williams (our quarterback), then Doug will call the play to the team in the huddle. This way I can hear what you're calling without having to understand these signals."

We tried this system but lost the next two games. "Okay, Joe," Coach said, "I can tell *you* are not comfortable calling the plays from the sidelines. I want you to go up to the coaches' booth and phone the play down to an assistant coach. He can repeat the call to a player who will take the play into the quarterback, who will then repeat the play to the team."

Now let's think about the real-time mechanics of this system. I've got to call the play through to the headset to one of my assistants. He then gives it to the wide receiver. One of our typical plays was "Trips Right Fake Zoom Liz 585 F Cross Sneak." You can only imagine giving this play to a receiver who's already been hit in the head a few times. The next game I barely recognized three plays we called. In the immortal words of the warden from the movie *Cool Hand Luke*, what we had at Tampa Bay that season was a bona fide "failure to communicate."

To me this illustration reinforces the extraordinary nature of the Bible. There is no miscommunication within its pages. Though written by more than forty men over 1,500 years, it remains our perfect playbook for the game of life. Two thousand years later the Bible provides clear insight and guidance to those who seek it. This book is a miracle book that had to be God inspired.

The Bible also brings God closer to us — in our times of need and in times of prosperity: "Yet you are near, LORD, and all your commands are true. Long ago I learned from your statutes that you established them to last forever" (Psalm 119:151 – 152). When we are desperate, the Holy Spirit communicates to us through God's Word that we are not alone. When we are flying high, we are reminded to keep things in perspective. The stories of great men and women like David and Ruth serve as guideposts for us; the gospel tells us the good news of Jesus Christ. What a playbook!

I'm just your "average Joe," and like you, I'm looking for practical tools to help me get through life. The Bible is the most practical and valuable resource I have in my possession. I've learned to turn to it daily and find it always lights my path — no matter how good or bad things are going for me. My hope is that you will learn this truth for yourself.

> *Dear Father, thank You for Your playbook, the Bible. Please help me to learn to turn to it during good and bad times. Help me realize that within its pages are the exact plays, guidance, and encouragement I need to win in the game of life. Amen.*

THE PERFECT GAME PLAN

"For I know the plans I have for you," declares the LORD,
"plans to prosper you and not to harm you,
plans to give you hope and a future."
JEREMIAH 29:11

Focused on the video breakdowns of the most successful runs against next week's opponent, I was startled to hear the rumbling garbage trucks begin-  ning their pickup right outside our window at Redskin Park. I glanced at my watch — it was already 3 a.m. This was a typical Monday at the end of a long day that included grading our game film, reviewing the film with our players, directing a light workout with the team, having a mandatory meeting with the media, and doing our TV interviews. You'd think the coaching staff would be

worn out and exhausted from Sunday's game and this grueling routine. But knowing those Monday late-night film
studies would have a lot to do with our final game plan for
that week, I typically felt a rush of adrenaline as we studied
our next opponent, trying to pinpoint strengths and weak-
nesses; it wasn't until late in the week after our game plan
was completed that the lack of sleep caught up with me.

On Wednesdays we'd give each player his playbook for
the next game. Then we'd practice the plays — defenses and
strategies for the rest of the week. As coaches we wanted
our players to have the best possible advantage that would
increase our chances for a win.

I believe this is what God does for us. As driven as I was
to craft the best plan for our players and as hard as I worked
to help my players be their best, would it make any sense
for us to believe that our Head Coach — God — would not
provide us with the perfect playbook for a winning strategy
for our biggest game of all — the game of life? He has done
that in His Word, the Bible. Our all-powerful, all-knowing,
and all-loving God has prepared the perfect game plan for
you and me. But are we diligently studying it?

You will find the locker room on game day is a quiet and
intense setting. The players are getting taped and making
equipment adjustments, and many players get to the locker
room two to three hours before they appear for warm-ups
on the field. Most of them are studying their game plans in
this final preparation for the game. You could cut the in-
tensity in the locker room with a knife.

In studying the Bible, do you and I make a similar
commitment to preparation? At one point in my life, I decided I would invest in real estate. At that point, I was not
studying what my Bible had to say about finances. As I

have detailed in my book *Game Plan for Life* and on other pages in this devotional, this decision led to one of the biggest messes I've ever experienced. I was playing the game without studying the game plan!

As I discovered later, God knew we were going to struggle with finances, and He has laid out financial principles to guide us in our decisions. As a matter of fact, God speaks about finances in His Word more than any other subject.

How about you? Are you seriously studying your game plan? What decisions in your life are you considering? Learn from my mistakes. Ask God to lead you in a study to determine the right direction for your life.

Heavenly Father, You are the coach of my life. I know that You love me and want what's best for me. You care for me so much that You have created a perfect game plan so that I can win the most important game I will play — the game of life. Please help me to seek You and learn Your game plan for my life. Amen.

COURAGE FOR THE WILD RIDE

*Now, Lord, consider their threats and enable your servants
to speak your word with great boldness.*
ACTS 4:29

Standing in the infield as our #20 Home Depot car barrel-rolled seven times, I witnessed one of the most spectacular wrecks I'd seen in all my years of NASCAR competition. Do-

ver International Speedway is nicknamed the Monster Mile for good reason — the banks of the turns are three stories high from top to bottom and cars come into them at speeds over 150 miles per hour. It is a punishing track that can destroy cars and test the nerves of even the most experienced racer. Our rookie driver, Joey Logano, was in that car as it finally ground to a stop on the track apron.

When Joey stepped up to the Sprint Cup series to drive for us, he was all of nineteen years old. We knew he was a talented driver and a stand-up young man — he'd gone through our driver development program, and in the process we also got to know Joey's family. He was ready for NASCAR's top-tier circuit. But one quality that you don't get many opportunities to measure in an individual is personal courage; this wreck in late September gave me an insight into the fortitude of that young man.

After he was freed from the car, Joey was taken to the infield infirmary. Though badly shaken up, he didn't have any injuries. "It just scared the heck out of me," he said when I got there. "That was the wildest ride I've ever been on. You can't go on a roller coaster any wilder than that." He was smiling in the post-accident interviews, but I could tell he'd been rattled.

As a rookie, we would have let him take a pass on his next race, but talking through the wreck and its impact on his confidence, he thought it was important to get right back into a car and drive the next week. You know what? Joey made quite a statement to the NASCAR community by winning his very next race on the following Saturday.

Life can be a "wild ride" at times. To me, one of the greatest acts of courage is to stand up, brush yourself off, and keep moving forward after a setback. Peter and the apostles gave us a great example of this after the crucifixion, resurrection, and ascension of Jesus.

Peter and John showed such courage when on the way to the temple to pray, they stopped to address a lame beggar who sat by the temple gates every day to collect handouts. Peter told the beggar he didn't have money to give but something more valuable. Then he commanded the man to stand up and be healed in the name of Jesus. The man became physically whole again and went about praising God. The Pharisees weren't happy to have a guy running around healed by a miracle of Christ's power, so they threw Peter and John into jail. They released the apostles the next day but not before intense questioning. What was the verdict of the interrogation? We read in Acts 4:13: "When they saw the courage of Peter and John and realized that they were unschooled, ordinary men, they were astonished and they took note that these men had been with Jesus." We also read that "many who heard the message believed" (Acts 4:4).

Now Peter and John had just come from a night in jail. More important, they knew that Christ had been mercilessly crucified and the Pharisees didn't want the power of His resurrection being preached. What did Peter and John do? They got up, brushed themselves off, and kept preaching Christ. That took real courage, especially after they saw firsthand what had happened to Jesus.

Where do you need courage to keep moving forward in your own life? Maybe you've just gotten through a problem in a relationship that has shaken your trust in others. Maybe your business failed or you've lost your job. Perhaps your health is concerning you. Call on the God who gives ordinary men extraordinary courage. He will give you the courage you require.

Dear Father, I confess to You that I am not always courageous. I look around at circumstances before me and can become fearful. Please give me the courage that Peter and John displayed after the crucifixion of Christ to continue doing what they were called to do — preach the gospel to a fallen world. Help me to have the courage to move forward in my life and to trust the outcome to You. Amen.

LEARNING FROM FINANCIAL DISASTER

*Do not be one who shakes hands in pledge or puts up
security for debts; if you lack the means to pay,
your very bed will be snatched from under you.*
PROVERBS 22:26 – 27

On other pages in this devotional, I share with you that coaching is a high-pressure profession and you're really

only as valuable as your last win. A great season might buy you a little more time but not much. Because of this, when Pat and the boys were younger, I really put a lot of pressure on myself to create financial security for our family. So even after my second Super Bowl win (XXII), I spent a lot of time listening to pitches and schemes that seemed to be "no brainers," just too good to pass up without participating. One such "opportunity" I jumped on nearly drove us to financial ruin. It also drove me to my knees and taught me a valuable life lesson.

A partnership was building homes and apartments in Oklahoma during the heart of the oil boom. That partnership would build and market the properties. All I had to do was pay the closing costs. We'd lease the properties until we sold each unit for a profit, and the rental fees would more than cover our expenses.

This was my kind of deal because I really didn't have to focus on it and I thought my liability was limited. "Joe, don't worry," one of the partners told me, "before you lose a dime, we'll lose everything we own." Guess what? They did! And I almost did, too.

For a couple of years we could hardly keep up with the demand, but soon enough, the Oklahoma economy collapsed and our investment went in the tank. I was back in D.C. trying to win the next Super Bowl when late notices from banks started arriving at my home. Turns out I had agreed to become part of a simple partnership and was equally liable for any loan commitments the partnership made. As I wrapped up the Redskins season, my friend Don Meredith (not the NFL quarterback/announcer Don Meredith) went out to investigate. We were devastated at what he discovered: through the partnership I was on the hook for millions of dollars!

As soon as I could, I flew out to meet with Don. One of the lowest points in my life was that first night at my hotel in Oklahoma. I remember getting down on my knees with tears rolling down my face and confessing to God I'd been a fool — I was playing the financial game without studying the game plan (God's Bible). I had completely let down Pat and the boys.

I didn't feel I should file for bankruptcy. I owed this money. I prayed, "God, You know I don't have the resources, so only You can straighten this out. Please show me what to do and I'll do it." I had been a fool, blinded by the possibilities of creating easy wealth.

From that point forward I resolved to do my best to understand and live by biblical financial principles. I individually contacted all of the creditors of the partnership, admitted my mistakes, and sought out a creative way to make the payments. Nine different banks were involved. It took me a long time and the valuable help of close friends and financial experts, but through God's grace, we paid off all of the loans, and Pat and I didn't have to file for bankruptcy.

The great news for us is that no matter how big the mess we make in life, if we are on God's team there is no mess that He cannot conquer. There were more miraculous events that came out of this calamity, but the biggest lesson I learned was that I needed to understand God's plan for my money, His biblical principles of stewardship. I broke a fundamental command by pledging myself as a security that I couldn't possibly pay back.

What are your financial burdens and challenges? Perhaps you've cosigned a loan with someone and you really couldn't afford to pay it back if you had to do so? I challenge you to learn the basics of financial management from the Bible. It's all in there, and it works. Or you can check out my book *Game Plan for Life.* Chapter 9 on finances should be helpful to you. The fact that God mentions finances in His Word over 2,000 times shows His desire to provide us with the right financial game plan.

Father, help me to have the right perspective on finances. I need to diligently study the financial principles You've laid out in Your Word. Help me prayerfully to seek Your direction with my financial decisions. Amen.

CREATION AND COMMON SENSE

For you created my inmost being;
you knit me together in my mother's womb.
I praise you because I am fearfully and wonderfully made;
your works are wonderful, I know that full well.
PSALM 139:13 – 14

My first memory of school dates back to elementary school in Sand Hill, North Carolina. I still recall the brick building  and the well-oiled hardwood floors along with the small school desks. I also remember the first big decision I had to make in life. I was nine and my elementary school teacher was teaching me that I was an accident of nature. I didn't claim to be the sharpest kid in the class, but this description of life didn't make a lot of sense to me. *Hey*, I thought to myself, *two amoebas happen to hit in a muddy puddle of water two billion years ago, and I was the result?*

My mother and grandmother, on the other hand, had a different view. They made sure that I was in church every Sunday morning, where my Sunday school teacher taught something totally opposite from what I was being taught in school. She pointed out the Scriptures in God's Word that described His creation of the world and His knitting me together in my mother's womb.

As I thought about these two theories, it became an easy decision for me. I knew I wasn't an accident, and it was therefore easy to believe there was a loving God who had created this world, created me, and wanted to have a personal relationship with me. I can remember at a morning church service stepping out in the aisle, walking forward, and telling the pastor that I knew I wasn't an accident and that I wanted to have a personal relationship with my Lord and Savior. I accepted as truth the fact that God sent His only Son, Jesus, to this earth to be crucified on the cross for my sins.

When people ask my view of creation, I often use the example of my watch. When I ask people to look at it, everyone acknowledges that it is a relatively complicated piece of machinery. When I ask them if they believe there is a watchmaker, that's an easy decision for them to make. Where there is a watch, there has to be a watchmaker. None of us has seen him, but we all believe that he exists.

When we look around us at the wonderful ways the earth is created, the fact that we have trees that help create the oxygen that you and I breathe, that we have men and women with the ability to love each other — to me it is a commonsense deduction that where there is a world, there has to be a world maker. Thank You, Lord, for making us and for creating this beautiful earth that surrounds us and makes life possible.

> *Heavenly Father, throughout the Bible You make it clear that I am not a product of evolution, of chance and random happenings. Rather, I read from the first pages of Genesis to the last pages of Revelation that You created me with purpose and an eternal destiny. Help me to claim this incredible truth. Help me rely on Your Spirit of Truth, rather than man-made theories, to understand my origins. Help me have the courage of my convictions and not to worry what others might think. Father, thank You for creating me. Amen.*

LETTING GOD TAKE CONTROL OF YOUR VOCATION

"One lap to go! Jarrett pulls in front … I know he's gone to the floorboard, he can't give it any more. It's the Dale and Dale show. He's gonna make it. Dale Jarrett's gonna win the Daytona 500!" NASCAR legend and CBS sports announcer Ned Jarrett was describing his son Dale's stunning victory over Dale Earnhardt at the Daytona 500 in 1993. You can still see Ned and the  CBS crew calling the last laps of the race on YouTube. Our Interstate Batteries #18 car had just beaten the Intimidator by a split second.

We were floored. We didn't even know how to get to victory lane after the race. "I think we were all kind of looking for some help," Dale said later on. "I remember looking at Joe. His family and Norm Miller, owner of Interstate Batteries, were there, and we were all looking at each other, wondering what just happened."

Pat and I couldn't believe it. In celebration, our sons, Coy and J.D., were wrestling around on the infield with their friend Todd Meredith, who's dad, Don, helped me start the team. The boys had all been on the pit crew, just out of college. The first race of our second season, NASCAR's Super Bowl, and we finally won a race. Someone in the sports media wrote, "Joe Gibbs Racing was legitimized — and Norm Miller looked like a genius for taking a chance on an unproven organization."[2] What an understatement that was! Throughout my career, I've had to learn to trust the Lord and rely upon His guidance, but I faced no bigger vocational challenge than moving from the relatively ordered world of the NFL, which I knew so well, to a wild ride that NASCAR team ownership would turn out to be.

Just a couple of years earlier, after winning Super Bowl XXVI against the Bills, I had circled up Coy and J.D. to talk about what was next for our family. J.D. didn't want to get into coaching — he'd seen the life up close, and it wasn't for him. The boys suggested racing, and we all thought that'd be worth pursuing. The boys and I loved all sorts of motor sports — jet skis, go-karts, motocross bikes, drag racing, and street rods. I told the boys, "Let's try to convince your mother to let us pursue starting a race team." When I went in to ask Pat, her only question to me was, "You're not going to be the driver, are you?" Once I assured her that was not the case, Pat became really excited too. It was a big risk for us, but we prayed and felt it was God's leading for our family.

This decision led to some conversations with successful NASCAR owners such as Rick Hendrick and Richard Petty. Rick made his general manager, Jimmy Johnson, available to us, and with his help, we created a proposal and began our search for a sponsor. We identified four potential companies and began our process. Norm Miller was our second stop.

Our initial phone call with Norm went great and he asked us to come to Interstate headquarters in Dallas. When I hadn't heard back from Norm in a couple of days after our visit, I decided to call him; maybe he'd at least be interested in an associate sponsorship. "No, Joe," he told me, "our executive team talked about it. We've decided we're in for the full deal."

Our game plan for starting the race team was that my good friend and business partner, Don Meredith, would oversee the start-up operation with J.D. and seventeen other employees while I continued to coach the Redskins and Coy would follow his dream of playing football at Stanford. From this initial dream and through many prayers and God's leading, today we've won three Cup championships, and JGR has become home to over 400 employees.

My takeaway from all of this is that if God puts something on your heart, take the risk to go for it. The playbook says in Proverbs 16:3, 9: "Commit to the LORD whatever you do, and he will establish your plans ... In their hearts humans plan their course, but the LORD establishes their steps." As I look back on our race team start-up, I can see God's hands guiding our decisions.

I encourage you to seek God's direction if you're getting ready to attempt something big—and then hang on for the ride of your life.

> *Dear Heavenly Father, Your Word tells us that*
> *everything on this earth is Yours and that it is*
> *ultimately You who makes dreams come true.*
> *Help me trust in You to lead me. You are the*
> *fulfillment of everything good. Amen.*

A NEW ARRIVAL

*Start children off on the way they should go, and even
when they are old they will not turn from it.*
PROVERBS 22:6

Our phone started ringing at one o'clock in the morning.
Pat and I received the fantastic news that our eighth grandchild was due shortly. We dashed over to the hospital to be
with my son Coy and his wife, Heath-
er, and soon enough little Jett Randall
Gibbs showed up on the scene. I can't
tell you how thrilling his arrival was —
I mean, we have two boys and we'd
wound up with four grandkids in one
family and now four in the other. Hey,

as a dad watching our two sons grow up, I never expected
that! But here they were — two great fathers with outstand-
ing wives.

The excitement of the moment got to me a little bit. When I finally had some time with the proud new mom, I said, "Heather, I'll do anything for a fifth. You name it ... cars, trips, vacations!" My timing wasn't the best as the delivery experience was still fresh on her mind. Nonetheless, this was a time for celebration for the Gibbs family.

Standing there looking at that tiny baby as they cleaned him up under the heat lamp caused me to think about what had just taken place. Another human being had just come into the world. This extraordinary little child was certainly no accident of evolution. Just the opposite — he'd been created by the amazing God we serve. Just thinking about the complexity of Jett Randall's eyes with millions of receptacles in them to allow him to see, those tiny little fingers already able to grip something, the fact that a miniature heart and lungs were in that body and he was now able to breathe in oxygen ... To me, the "average Joe," the miracle of a human being is one of the commonsense proofs of God's existence.

Who knows? This little boy could turn out to be a man who changes the whole complexion of the world. Maybe he will help lead our country to revival. Maybe he will discover the cure for an incurable disease or be a dad himself and bring others into the world. But right now, here he lay, completely vulnerable on that small table. He was absolutely helpless to do anything without his mother or father and those who were going to love him by his side. God had given Jett Randall the miracle of life, but now the obligation was on his parents — and us as grandparents — to shape his conscience and give him the tools to live a meaningful life, to prepare him for the great works God has planned for him to accomplish (Ephesians 2:10).

King David gave us a great example of this with his son Solomon. David was a man after God's own heart, and he had a great work that he wanted to do — to build God a magnificent temple that would house the ark of the covenant and display to all mankind the God he served. Yet God told David this was not to be his achievement. He had been a man of war. Rather, God would let David's son Solomon build the temple (2 Samuel 7).

So what did David do? He prepared every single aspect of what God wanted done with his son (1 Chronicles 28:11 – 19). He shared his plan with Solomon and covered everything he envisioned would be in the temple — from how the courts and adjoining rooms were laid out to the specific materials craftsmen were to use — no detail was spared. Solomon followed through and built the temple. It glorified God and was so amazing that rulers of other kingdoms would come to marvel at it and to meet King Solomon who had built it.

How about you and me? What's our obligation to our kids and grandkids? We are to lead them into a personal relationship with Jesus Christ, and then we are to prepare them for God's desires for their life. We need to let them know that no one is an accident and to know the God who created them. As David did for his son Solomon, we are to set our children on the right course to accomplish His purpose for them on this earth.

Heavenly Father, thank You for commonsense signs of Your creation, from the miracle of the human body to the birth of a child. Help me prepare those You have given me so that they may know You and accomplish Your purposes on earth. Amen.

CHANGE THAT IMPACTS OTHERS

*He who began a good work in you will carry it on
to completion until the day of Christ Jesus.*
PHILIPPIANS 1:6

The memorial service for Sean Taylor was powerful. He was our twenty-four-year-old star safety who died defending his family from a break-in at his house. The pews were

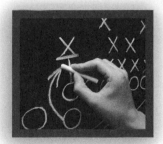

packed with Redskins and his former teammates from the University of Miami. Though there were a lot of tough players and coaches at that memorial, there were few, if any, dry eyes in the house. The service was a great testimony to a young man's life, and it impacted many who attended.

When we drafted Sean as a Redskin in the first round, he was very distant that first year. In some ways, he was disrespectful and even angry. But Sean's fourth year at Redskin Park was remarkable, not only because of the caliber of his play — *Sports Illustrated* named him one of the ten hardest hitters in the NFL that year — but also because of the change we saw in him. As a teammate, a father, and a man, it was obvious to me and those closest to Sean that something was at work in his heart. It started when his little daughter was born, and the impact continued after his death. I believe it led to change in many other lives.

Pastor Brett Fuller, one of our Redskins chaplains and the man who spent the most time helping Sean understand the Bible and how to live the Christian life, told me that in the two days following Sean's memorial, thirteen individuals from the Redskins organization asked for appointments to talk about their faith and important issues in their lives. They, like many of us, had been shocked by Sean's passing and the reminder of how fragile life can be. Sudden tragedy like this has a way of making us take measure of that which is most important in our lives, where we should focus our attention, what we should change.

I find myself playing in the fourth quarter of life, and the thing that amazes me the most has been how fast my life has gone by. My oldest grandson, Jackson, is fourteen years old. It was a shock for me to realize I now have a grandson who is a teenager. But even this late in the game the Lord is constantly working on me, encouraging me to change and be a better husband, father, and leader. He is challenging me to focus on the legacy I'll leave behind and the impact my life will have on others, especially my family. As tragic and devastating as the death of Sean Taylor was to those of us who knew him, for me, his will always be a story of the positive changes I saw in a young and amazingly gifted athlete and the impact his life had on others.

Maybe you're struggling with sin or other personal challenges in your own life and wonder if you can truly change. Believe me, our enemy, Satan, would love for you to think change is impossible. But the truth is that our Lord is in the business of changing us for the better. There was only one perfect person in the history of the world, Jesus Christ. The rest of us are works in progress, people who need continual improvements. The Lord worked in Sean Taylor's life, He's working in Joe Gibbs' life, and He can work in yours.

Heavenly Father, I know that there are some areas in my life that need to change, that I can be a better person to those whom You've placed in my life and create a lasting impact. Give me the faith to trust that You can change me and that You will continue to help me conform to the model that Your Son, Jesus Christ — the only perfect person to ever walk the face of the earth — provides for me. Amen.

OUR GOD OF SECOND CHANCES

Blessed is the one whose transgressions are forgiven,
whose sins are covered.
PSALM 32:1

"I want to be an example," said Robert, "and hopefully change someone's life in the near future." These are powerful words considering Robert's current status. Convicted of murder, he will be in prison for the rest of his life. He is only forty-nine. Now, even behind bars, he wants to have a positive impact on others.

Jerome is getting ready to leave prison in a year. "We're not inmates; we're not criminals," he said. "We are brokenhearted men who have lost our direction, but today we find our destiny." He and hundreds of his fellow prisoners at a correctional institute in South Carolina, all

48 GAME PLAN FOR LIFE

wearing their tan jumpsuits, had come out in the heat to hear us talk about God's game plan for life.

On the Saturday before the Daytona 500, I had the chance to speak to hundreds of inmates at the Central Florida Reception Center — a nice-sounding name for a correctional facility just outside of Orlando. The warden even let a group of local Harley Davidson riders bring their bikes in the yard, so the prisoners could check them out, which made it a more interesting visit.

One of the most rewarding ministry opportunities for me in the last few years has been speaking to prisoners. I can truthfully tell you that in the hundreds, maybe thousands, of men I've encountered, not one has been disrespectful. Most listen carefully. They make eye contact. They listen. They are serious about making the most of their situations. Many have made commitments to follow Christ.

What's the message I share with prisoners? The real message to these guys is that we serve a God of second chances. It's that simple. When we repent, He forgives us of our sins. The fact is, these men are in prison because their mistakes were big enough for them to end up incarcerated. But to be honest, I've made some pretty big mistakes in my life, too. Haven't you? We all need to be forgiven and given a second chance.

After winning our second Super Bowl in 1988, Chuck Colson asked me to join him on a visit to inmates at nearby Lorton Penitentiary, which at that time housed some of the most violent criminals in the D.C. area. At first I was somewhat apprehensive, but soon the place was rocking with hooting and hollering — the guys were happy to have me there after the Redskins' recent victory over the Denver

Broncos. We spent time with men on death row and in the AIDS ward. I was impressed with Chuck's courage as he took the hand of each man and prayed with him, especially back then when we really didn't know much about AIDS or how it was spread.

I still work with Prison Fellowship founded by Chuck. Chuck was a great example of the power of second chances. He rose to the highest levels of power in Washington, D.C., becoming a counselor to a president; he then was sent to prison on Watergate-related charges. In prison, he saw that prisoners needed spiritual guidance as well as practical training to succeed in life. His outreach has touched the lives of thousands of prisoners and their families.

Perhaps the clearest picture we have of God giving second chances is found in the story of King David. Besides Jesus, David is probably one of the most loved figures in the Bible. In Acts 13:22 we read, "God testified concerning him: 'I have found David son of Jesse, a man after my own heart; he will do everything I want him to do.'"

What mistakes did David make? Big ones. He cheated on one of his soldiers, Uriah the Hittite, getting his wife pregnant. Then to cover his sin, he had Uriah positioned in battle so that he would surely be killed (2 Samuel 11).

And what did David do when confronted with his sin? He threw himself at the feet of God and asked for forgiveness. God sees our hearts, and He is quick to forgive us our sins when we repent. Psalms 32 and 51, written by David, speak to the amazing grace that comes when we ask forgiveness for our sins.

I believe that one of the most appealing messages of Christianity is that we can be forgiven and that we serve a God of second chances. Have you embraced this truth in your life? Do you find yourself needing a second chance? If you are struggling, reading about David's life in God's Word could be helpful to you.

> *Dear Lord, we all need second chances at some point in our lives. Our sin, just like David's, brings us down and encumbers us. Help me to identify the sin in my life that I need to make right with You. Give me the grace to seek Your forgiveness and be truly free. Help me share the message of Your mercy with those that need to hear it. Amen.*

NOT COMPROMISING OUR BELIEFS

Be strong and very courageous.
Be careful to obey all the law my servant Moses gave you;
do not turn from it to the right or to the left,
that you may be successful wherever you go.
JOSHUA 1:7

At each race, the driver and the pit crews wear fire suits emblazoned with the logos of our sponsors. When we win a race, afterward the driver does his victory burnout and makes it over to the winners circle. He and the rest of the team, including me, go through what's called the "hat dance" — we take multiple pictures of the team celebrating the victory, each time wearing a different sponsor's ball cap. We are proud of the companies that support our racing and work really hard to help them promote their products and services.

Not too long ago I was attending the annual marketing summit we hold at Joe Gibbs Racing headquarters when an issue came up that challenged me to take a stand. During these corporate gatherings, each of our sponsors shares how it uses motorsports to enhance its brand and sell products and services. Then our executive team makes a presentation highlighting how we try to maximize our sponsor's marketing dollars. These forums are great for our financial partners as well as our staff as they lead more effective marketing and better customer relationships.

During one particular presentation by an energy drink producer, the presenters declared that their product enhanced sexual performance and then showed a sexually suggestive video. Everyone in the auditorium became uneasy and embarrassed. It was completely inappropriate.

Following that presentation I suggested we all take a break and asked the three representatives from the drink company to meet in my office. I let the guys know how disappointed and uncomfortable I was by their presentation and made it clear that even though their company was an important financial partner with the race team, it was obvious to me that we could no longer do business together. I then phoned the CEO and explained the reasons for my decision.

Upon returning to the marketing summit I shared the news with our other corporate partners. There was a strong sense of relief in the room, and many individuals came up to me afterward to express their support and appreciation of the decisive action we took.

Many times in life we are confronted with decisions that require us to take a moral stand. In some cases it can seem really costly — such as in this situation. But I've honestly found that if our intent is to honor God, He blesses such decisions. In this particular situation He led us to other racing sponsors who fit with our company values and turned into long-term financial partners.

Maybe you're facing a challenge like this — it could be a decision that will cost you financially. I hope this personal challenge that I just shared with you will encourage you to seek God's direction, lean on His guidance, and ultimately take the stand you need to take.

Dear Heavenly Father, because Your Son, Jesus Christ, was fully man and fully God, He knows how tempting it is for us to compromise. Yet when we do, we hurt not only ourselves, but also those who might be watching and hoping to see something different about us. Please give me the strength to overcome the desire to compromise. Help me to trust that You'll bless the decisions that we make following Your biblical principles. Amen.

MAKING BIG DECISIONS IN LIFE

*Trust in the LORD with all your heart and lean not on
your own understanding; in all your ways submit to him,
and he will make your paths straight.*
PROVERBS 3:5 – 6

In 2007 the Redskins made the first-round playoffs, facing the Seahawks in Seattle. I was convinced that our team had

a good shot of making it to the Super Bowl. We'd won the last four games of the regular season against very tough teams — the Bears, Giants, Vikings, and Cowboys — and our practices for the first post-season game had gone really well.

We took a 14 – 13 lead in the fourth quarter, and I thought to myself that I'd never been in a stadium this loud in thirty years of coaching. The crowd was excited, pulling for the Seahawks. I was certainly excited too because at this point in the game, our guys had fought extremely hard in a hostile stadium. But our lead slipped away and we eventually lost 35 – 14.

When I finally escaped to the quiet of the flight home to Washington, I had a chance to reflect. I was extremely disappointed because I felt like we'd ended the regular season playing some of the best football I'd ever coached. It was certainly a downer knowing that after all we had fought for all year, the season was over.

Once we finished our team physicals, I had my final meeting with the team on Monday and then a meeting with our owner, Dan Snyder. I told him I was going home to Charlotte to visit with the family for a few days and then I would be back.

The truth was, I was beginning to really think about the next football season and how much of a commitment coaching an NFL team demanded from me. I still had one year left on my contract, but I felt the decision to coach another year was something I needed to evaluate. During the season a coach's personal life is so hard. And the 2007 season had been one of my toughest in football. We had faced the loss of Sean Taylor, our star defensive safety. It was hard to go through something like that; it had never happened before in my career, and obviously it was something you can never be prepared for. And yet, to see our team rally at the end of the season made it one of my most rewarding experiences in coaching.

Maybe you are facing a similar decision right now in your own life. If so, I'd like to share something with you. Over the years Pat and I have made some big decisions and developed a formula for handling them.

First, you need to be in prayer. During these times make sure you are seeking God's counsel in talking to Him and listening to Him in your quiet times of meditation. Second, you must make time for solid Bible study. I can't tell you how many times I've found the answers I needed as I was studying my Bible during my daily devotionals.

Seeking godly counsel is also important. The Bible talks about surrounding yourself with wise counselors, of having people in your life to whom you are accountable — someone who can look you in the eyes and say, "That's a good idea," or "I don't think that's a good move for you." And if you listen carefully and are willing to hear, you just might hear the voice of God speaking through your spouse and other close advisors. If you're married, God has put that person in your life, and I've found that when Pat and I agree on decisions, we have never made a bad one.

The more I talked, prayed, sought godly counsel, and studied God's Word, it once again became evident to me that my decision should be to step down from the Redskins and go back home and be with family. I can honestly tell you that a peace started to come over me that I had made the right decision.

Are you trusting in the Lord and leaning on Him for your understanding and direction? It starts with daily Bible reading and prayer time. It might take you a little while to build this habit, but I can tell you it is well worth the comfort and peace God provides.

Heavenly Father, thank You so much for Your
love and the way you guide my steps and make
my paths straight. Help me to be faithful in my

communication and relationship building with
You. When times are unclear, let me learn to
lean on You and not my own understanding.
Amen.

NOTHING IS TOO BIG FOR GOD

For what god is there in heaven or on earth who can do the deeds and mighty works you do?
DEUTERONOMY 3:24

It was Sunday morning and I was in Washington, D.C., sitting in a condo complex listening to a counselor's eight-year-old daughter read to me from her storybook. I had gone downtown to meet with some young at-risk teenagers that were transitioning through the court system. These young men were all being assigned to some form of correctional institute. After this young girl finished reading to us, one of the teenage boys in the program walked up to me with tears in his eyes and said, "I wouldn't be in this situation if I could read."

As I researched his background, I found that he had no family and had committed a number of petty crimes and found himself waiting to be assigned to a correctional facility. Falling behind in education, he had lost his ability to compete in society and wanted a second chance.

This is just one of the young people who made a big impression on me that day. I came to the realization that these young men needed more than just an hour or two on Sunday morning. They needed 24/7 love, discipline, godly principles, and an education to compete in society.

I asked three friends to join me in a discussion about how to help young people struggling in these types of life situations. One of the ideas that came out of this first meeting was the possibility of building a youth home in the D.C. area. Using private funds, we could serve at-risk kids ages fourteen to eighteen and try and equip them for life. We decided to step out in faith and have a banquet to raise funds.

We raised about $130,000 and put down a deposit on a 130-acre piece of property in Manassas, Virginia. After that, we had about $70,000 left in the bank. I went to see a friend of mine, Bill Hazel, who owned a large construction company. I laid out the plans we had drawn up for the youth home. After spending a few minutes looking them over, he told me the dirt work on this project would be about $700,000. I was totally taken aback and didn't know what to say. Bill said, "Don't worry about this. I am going to make sure we get this done."

As we mentioned this project to others in the community, their reaction was similar to Bill's. People heard about it and wanted to contribute in a number of ways. And can you believe it? We actually got the home built. Today that home serves somewhere between fifty and seventy-five girls and boys. We have a year-round school where we can double a normal school year. We added a gym to our school complex and we added girls' homes in 2000.

As I think about the youth home today, I am aware that we had to step out in faith for this project. There's no way we could have done it on our own. Only God could and did do it. But what if we hadn't taken that first step?

How about you? Do you feel God telling you to attempt something? I wonder how many times I have failed to step out when God has asked me to. That is one of my prayers going forward—God give me the courage when I sense Your desire for me to attempt something big.

You may be in a situation where you feel as if God is encouraging you to attempt something, but when you look at the circumstances all around it, you think it is too big for you. I encourage you to believe that if God is telling you to do something, nothing is too big for Him.

Heavenly Father, thank You for allowing me to participate in Your ministry here on earth. Give me the courage to follow Your leading. Help me to look to You and Your boundless capabilities, rather than to me with my human limitations. Amen.

LIFE IS A TEAM SPORT

Though one may be overpowered,
two can defend themselves.
A cord of three strands is not quickly broken.
ECCLESIASTES 4:12

When asked to speak at a prayer breakfast or corporate event, I usually get questions about teams and team build-ing. My whole professional life I have been involved in selecting the right people and then asking them to set aside their own individual goals and focus on the goals of their team. Why is this so hard? It goes against their human nature.

We come into the world self-centered. I can illustrate that with the birth of our first grandchild, Jackson. For the first couple of years, he was an only child. Every toy was his. But two years later his brother came on the scene, and Jackson didn't like the idea that he was going to have to share.

Great teams are made up of people willing to sacrifice their individual goals for the goals of the team. Football is a great example of a team sport. All you have to do is look into that a quarterback's eyes when he goes to the line of scrimmage and sees those defensive players getting ready to try and kill him. He is counting on his teammates to protect him.

The way I see it, the game of life is the same. Although our ultimate success is guaranteed when we commit ourselves to Jesus, the other players on our team are crucial to how well we play. So when I'm asked to talk about teams, I usually share a personal story from my early career.

The '83 Redskins were one of the best teams ever assembled in professional football — in my opinion and in the opinions of some of the sports media. Proven veterans led the squad, setting a number of records, including most points scored in a season and an NFL record of +43 turnover ratio. We had just won a big game at RFK Stadium, and we were going down to play the hated Dallas Cowboys for the divisional title. As I sat at the breakfast table on Monday morning preparing to go to work and reading the good press in the newspaper, I was feeling pretty good about myself.

Then out of the blue, I heard my wife, Pat, tell me, "Do you mind picking up your bathrobe and socks?" The nerve of her speaking to such an important person in this way!

No matter what I was thinking, I also knew how to get along with Pat and I picked up my bathrobe and socks. Then Pat began to share some things about J.D. and Coy that she thought I needed to know. I found myself thinking, *Doesn't she know what I have got to do this week? Hadn't she read the papers?* As we find ourselves doing sometimes, I stormed out of the house, slamming the door behind me.

Fortunately, I'd made a promise to myself that I'd try to pray on the drive into Redskin Park each morning. About halfway to work it dawned on me. My pride had got the best of me, and I knew that I needed to humble myself and apologize to my teammate. When I got into the office, I called Pat and said, "Mom, I want you to know, what you're taking care of at home — our two boys, J.D. and Coy — is more important than what I'm taking care of at work." I thanked her and asked for forgiveness for my attitude at breakfast.

You see, the world sells us a bill of goods as we play the game of life: the way to be successful is to make money, to excel at your career, or, in my case, to win football games. Yet the most important things Pat and I are going to leave on this earth are our two boys and our influence on others. As important as my job seemed to me at that time, it was not going to have the eternal impact my relationships could. (Anyway, I'm convinced a few years from now I'll be sitting in an old-folks home with a bunch of other old guys telling them I coached the Washington Redskins, and they'll be telling the nurses, "Get this nut out of here. He thinks he coached the Washington Redskins.")

God gave me the perfect teammate when I married Pat. If I'm flying high and mighty, she has a way of bringing me back to reality ("Go pick up your socks, Joe!"); when I'm at rock bottom, she's always helped me find the strength to move forward. Proverbs 18:22 says, "He who finds a wife finds what is good and receives favor from the LORD."

In the game of life, if you're married, your spouse is your most valuable teammate. Is this true in your relationship?

Father, in the game of life, You've put other players on my team to help me play the best I possibly can. Thank You for giving me the perfect mate for me. Help me to value her and honor her role as the most valuable player on my team. Amen.

▶ Photo taken at Redskin Park in January 2004, the day the announcement was made that Joe was returning as head coach of the Washington Redskins after leaving 12 years prior.

▲ Joe, JD, and Coy Gibbs in the lobby of JGR Headquarters with Yamaha Motocross team bike.

▶ Joe on the sidelines before a Washington Redskins home game in 2005.

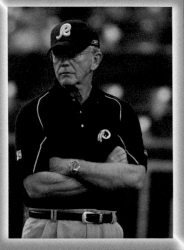

◄ Coach at Pocono

► Joe celebrating 20 years of Joe Gibbs Racing from 1991 to 2011.

'91 TWENTY YEARS '11

JGR driver, Denny Hamlin, wins at Martinsville Speedway in October 2009 for the 3rd time in his career and is joined in Victory Lane by the Gibbs Family. Left to right: Joe Gibbs, Hamlin, JD Gibbs, Jackson Gibbs.

◀ Joe listening to Nationwide race in the Homestead-Miami Speedway pits.

▶ Joe speaks to prison inmates at Central Florida Reception Center in Orlando, Florida.

GR Driver, Kyle Busch, Wins 2009 Nationwide Championship at Homestead-Miami Speedway. Left to right: Joe Gibbs, JD Gibbs, Busch, Jason Ratcliff, Crew Chief.

▲ 2010 team photo in front of Joe Gibbs Racing Headquarters, Huntersville, North Carolina.

STORMS OF LIFE

So keep up your courage, men,
for I have faith in God that it will happen
just as he told me.
ACTS 27:25

The NASCAR inspector walked over to our crew chief, Dave Rogers, and informed him that Kyle Busch's winning Toyota had not passed post-race inspection. Dave was shocked. After every race NASCAR inspects the top race finishers and randomly selects several other cars in the field. In this particular case the right front of our #18 car was too low, so we didn't pass inspection. 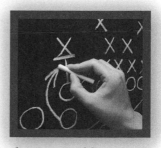 When this happens the team gets docked points and has to pay a fine. For us, that meant losing six points and paying $25,000, plus having to put up with bad press.

Back in Charlotte at our race shop we tried everything we could to duplicate what might have happened to make the car fail inspection — maybe it was heat buildup from all of the braking during the race. Trying as hard as we could, we couldn't replicate the problem to find what actually caused the variance. It was a real head scratcher, but the bottom line for us was that it was just one of the things that can happen to you in racing. You take the penalty and move on to the next race.

Fast-forward a week later to Michigan International Speedway. Leaving the Pocono penalty behind us, we were excited about going to Michigan because we had recently experienced great success there.

At the race shop, before traveling to Michigan, we had an in-depth technical discussion about a new oil pan our engineers had designed for our motors. Our whole technical team met to discuss race strategy, and when discussion turned to the new oil pan, not a man in the room thought NASCAR would have a problem with it; so we went ahead and installed it on all three cars. We felt it was a better piece of equipment that could improve our on-track performance, and we looked forward to testing the new technology at Michigan. We had made the decision not to go through the longer part approval process where we'd send the part to NASCAR to examine. But we had no doubt that NASCAR would see the new oil pan when it inspected the cars prior to the race.

We arrived at Michigan, and after going through pre-race inspection, guess what? NASCAR didn't like the new design. In fact, we were told to take the oil pans off the cars. NASCAR didn't believe the parts were illegal, but it deemed them to be different enough that they should have been submitted for review prior to using them on a racecar. We'd blown it — I'd blown it. You see, I had been in that technical meeting where we all made a pretty serious miscalculation. One week after being penalized at Pocono, here we were again — two weeks and two infractions of the NASCAR rules. NASCAR fined us again and placed our crew chiefs and car chiefs on probation. This situation really hit me hard.

Standing on the starting grid that week, obviously depressed, I asked myself, "Why is this happening to me?" But in my Bible study in Acts that week, I found that Paul also had some serious adversity in his life, and he must have asked that same question. Paul had been imprisoned, survived a terrible shipwreck, only to end up back in prison again. I'm sure at some point Paul was asking himself, "Why is this happening to me?"

In Mark 4, there is another example of a literal storm when Jesus tells the disciples to get into a boat and cross over to the other side of the lake. That night they encountered a storm. Now think about this. Jesus knew ... what? He knew there was a storm out there. And yet He sent the disciples straight into it.

I stopped and thought about this for a while. Whether it was oil pans or other issues, there was no question that I would be facing storms in my life, and some of them were going to be extremely tough. What we know about God is that He is all-powerful and all-knowing, so He knows that, like the storm on the lake He sent the disciples into, we too will have challenges. But He does this to help us grow spiritually and to assure us He is always there for us.

How about you? Have you run into any storms in your life? Maybe you're in one right now. It may not be an oil pan issue with NASCAR, but maybe you're facing financial storms, relationship storms, or addiction storms. Whatever it might be, it's not too big for God. Sometimes He may send us into a storm, but it is to deepen our faith. When we see adversity appear in our lives, we can be assured that if we are on God's team, He is there with us. We should be praying to Him and asking His advice on how to negotiate these storms.

In my life, when I have come out on the other side of tough times, I've been amazed at how God has worked in these situations. As I look back on them, I see there are reasons He had me go through that experience. Chances are when you come out on the other side, you'll say the same thing to yourself.

> *Dear Lord, You know the storms I'm going through today. Humanly speaking, my tendency would be to run from this adversity. Please give me the strength to persevere through them and the wisdom to discern what You want me to learn through this experience. Help me be comforted by knowing You are there with me during this storm. Amen.*

REDEDICATING
MY LIFE

Do not conform to the pattern of this world,
but be transformed by the renewing of your mind.
Then you will be able to test and approve what
God's will is — his good, pleasing and perfect will.
ROMANS 12:2

Competing in two professional sports, I've been fortunate enough to be associated with some thrilling plays on the field and daring moves on the track.  Yet away from the stadium lights, some of the most exciting personal experiences I've had involved making career moves and starting new chapters in my vocational life. Probably the most well-known instance of this was in 1991, when I went from being in the NFL to NASCAR. (What was I thinking??) Less well-known, but still an exciting change for Pat and me, occurred twenty years earlier, in 1971, when we made the decision to leave Southern Cal where I was the offensive line coach and accept a similar position with the University of Arkansas. It turned out that this move would have a huge impact on my life.

Pat and I relocated with a great deal of anticipation. As a coach's wife, she was used to moving our family and quickly set about making our new home and life in Fayetteville. I immediately went on the road recruiting. Although I headed to Arkansas with my football career in mind, I was soon surrounded by a group of strong Christian men who were not only great at the game of football but were also great at the game of life. Two assistant coaches made a significant impact on me: Raymond Berry, the Hall of Fame Baltimore receiver who was coaching our receivers; and Don Breaux, a former NFL quarterback, who had coached with me at Florida State two years earlier and was now our quarterbacks coach.

Another man I met in Arkansas was fantastic at the game of life but had nothing to do with the game of football. George Tharel was the manager of the local J. C. Penney store and my Sunday school teacher. He wasn't athletic or physically imposing, yet he had tremendous stature with me. He loved the Lord and possessed incredible wisdom from a life lived trying to please God. We started a connection that would last until the end of his life.

These three men had something I wanted. Their relationships with their wives and children were solid, and they seemed to possess a deep confidence and self-assurance — a peace. I observed Raymond's dedicated walk with the Lord and was deeply impressed. Don Breaux's dramatic spiritual redirection of his life had really caught my attention. George Tharel's faithfulness, wisdom, and humility stood out to me. As I studied these men whom God had put in my path, I realized that even though I had a personal relationship with the Lord, I was definitely not living for Him.

At the early age of nine, I had made a commitment to invite Christ into my life as my Lord and Savior, but my college days and the first years of my coaching career didn't reflect this. Actually, I had been drifting away from the Lord. He was there as kind of a safety net for salvation but had little impact on my day-to-day living.

So it came about that one Sunday night at church in Fayetteville, Arkansas, I walked down the aisle and made this statement to the Lord: "I know that I have a personal relationship with You, but I must confess that I have not been living for You." I wish that I had always walked closely with the Lord, but the reality was that I had wasted many years by failing to seek His guidance in every part of my life. This was a turning point for me. This commitment to rededicate my life resulted in my walking closer with the Lord.

I wonder, as you read this devotional, if you find yourself in a similar situation. The decision I made to begin a closer walk with the Lord has been one of the most gratifying decisions of my life, and if you are feeling a distraction in your relationship with the Lord, I encourage you to take that step and rededicate your life.

Dear Lord, You do not desire me to conform to this world. Please keep me from drifting away from You. With the God of the entire universe willing to guide my every action and decision, help me to walk closely with You. Please forgive me for that portion of my life that I spent away from You, and I prayerfully ask You to direct my steps and keep me on Your path. Amen.

IMPORTANCE OF FAITHFUL RELATIONSHIPS

If your brother or sister sins, go and point out
their fault, just between the two of you.
If they listen to you, you have won them over.
But if they will not listen, take one or two others along,
so that "every matter may be established
by the testimony of two or three witnesses."
MATTHEW 18:15 – 16

We travel extensively in the world of motorsports. At Joe Gibbs Racing, we have been involved with six different series, and in all of them we find ourselves crisscrossing the country. On any given weekend, we may have 100 employees on the road. Though racing is exciting, travel like this can be grueling on our employees and hard on their families. It can also lead some individuals into serious temptation.

In one racing series we no longer participate in, we heard rumors that a valued employee — a leader and a man who was key in his role — was having an extramarital affair during race weekends when he was away from his wife. I've always said that any success we have as a racing team is because of our people, and part of my responsibilities as a coach/owner is to look out for our people. In this case, we had to confront the individual and let him know that his behavior was unacceptable. It was unhealthy for him, his family, and the people on our team looking to him as its leader. It also sent the wrong message to our sponsors about our company's integrity and commitment to excellence.

Though we hoped the behavior of this person would change after the warning, we soon learned that it hadn't, and we were confronted with a major leadership challenge. We decided to let the man go in the middle of the racing season. If one of our leaders was being deceptive in his closest relationship — with his wife — and we acted as if everything was okay, what did that say to him and the people we were responsible to lead?

The decision caused a lot of difficulty for our team. We lost a valuable team member and knew our performance would most likely take a hit on the racetrack. Some of our competitors and the media couldn't understand why we'd let a talented guy go in the middle of the season and tried to make some news out of it. But it was the right call. We had an obligation to this man and his family. Exposing a situation like this was not easy to do, but if we just turned our heads and said nothing, we might have missed an opportunity for this individual to make a change in his life.

Trying to hold a high standard in our culture is tough to do, but I believe the Bible makes it clear that it is our responsibility to do so. No matter what your occupational endeavor—running a large enterprise or running a family—you will often be challenged with situations where you know what the right thing to do is but are tempted to look the other way (James 4:17).

God is our head coach in the game of life, and the Bible is our playbook. There are standards to which we need to aspire, and they are in black and white, right in the Bible. Though it is difficult to make the hard call and do what is right in the eyes of the Lord, I believe He blesses us for doing it. In the end, the standards God gives us are for our protection and well-being.

Maybe you're aware of a situation at work that is immoral or wrong and you're tempted to do nothing. As hard as it might seem, pray for wisdom and see if God will lead you to do what is right. Not out of judgment but out of humility, that God might be honored and the situation redeemed for His glory. If you find yourself tempted or if you find yourself having committed a sin, God states in His Word that we can ask for forgiveness, and He will reinstate us to a right-standing relationship with Him.

Dear Father, thank You for being the Head Coach of my life and giving me the Bible as a playbook so I can know what to do to be successful and to avoid failure — what is good and pleasing to You and what is not (Ephesians 5:10). Please give me the strength to do what is right — not with pride and anger, but with humility and grace so that Your redemptive work might occur and that You might be glorified to all who are involved. Amen.

ALWAYS LISTEN TO YOUR WIFE

Houses and wealth are inherited from parents,
but a prudent wife is from the LORD.
PROVERBS 19:14

On other pages in this devotional and in my *Game Plan for Life* book, I've documented some of my financial struggles. For the most part, they involved me making a big mistake,

wandering from God's game plan for my finances, and then getting back on track by God's grace. Sometimes I'm a slow learner, and it took me a few stumbles to learn my lessons. From a relationship standpoint, one of the most important lessons I learned early

on was to listen to my wife, Pat. Until I nearly went bankrupt in the Oklahoma real estate deal, my practice had been to ask Pat her opinion, but if she didn't agree, to pester her until she came around to my view. Every time I did this, we met failure and lost money.

So a couple of years later, I chuckled to myself when a good friend of ours, a financial advisor, approached me about an investment in one of the wildest schemes I'd ever heard of — and I'd heard a lot of them! The idea consisted of us participating in an oil lease lottery. The winners would have control of valuable leases and could sell them to players in the oil industry. As he explained this to me, I told him that after my last fiasco, Pat and I had to agree on any more investments, and he'd have to sell the idea to Pat. So he asked to meet with Pat and me to present his concept.

Now to be truthful, I didn't think it had a prayer of succeeding with Pat — she's practical and had been through so much turmoil with my earlier investments. So you can bet I was surprised when she agreed to listen. "Sure. What can it hurt to listen?" she said.

The night I sat in my living room listening to this presentation, I almost laughed out loud. It sounded even more preposterous when I heard it again. This guy had zero chance with Pat.

When he finished, Pat turned to me and said, "I think we need to do this." I was in total shock. My conservative wife, who had gone through so much with my earlier financial schemes, was agreeing for us to take a risk on this one. And guess what? It worked. Two months later, we hit a winner and won a valuable lease that we were able to turn around and make a considerable financial gain on.

The lesson I learned here was to really listen to Pat's advice on big decisions. She was a loyal soldier, and she would follow me wherever, but God had put her in my life for more than that. When we were truly unified, our decisions were better and succeeded. When I badgered Pat into following me despite her better judgment, I failed.

How about you? Are you seeing your wife as a gift from the Lord and taking advantage of her wisdom, or do you try to railroad your big decisions through? I've learned that a lot of guys pretend to listen to their wives but in the end don't heed their counsel. My hope is that you don't make the same mistake I did and instead take the time to truly listen to the most important advisor the Lord has put in your life.

Dear Lord, thank You for the gift of marriage and providing me with the perfect partner. Help me to learn to listen to her and truly value her prudent counsel. Give me the humility to ask her forgiveness if I have not been a good listener. Thank You that You are the God of new beginnings and can help me change today. Amen.

WHOM DO YOU TRUST?

Truly I tell you, if you have faith as small as
a mustard seed, you can say to this mountain,
"Move from here to there," and it will move.
Nothing will be impossible for you.
MATTHEW 17:20

The night before every road game, the Redskins have a chapel service as a time for encouragement and Bible study. During a particularly rough stretch  my second time around with the Redskins, I asked a good friend of mine, Dr. Wendell Kempton, to conduct our service prior to playing the Saints in New Orleans. Wendell spent over thirty years as president of a missionary agency serving fifty countries and was also active in ministering to professional athletes and teams. The Saints were 9 – 4 while we were 4 – 9. Most of us were pretty anxious about the game. Since Wendell had done a great job sharing with our team before, I was really hoping he'd have an encouraging word for us.

"I met a man one time," said Wendell as he started to share, "and he told me he was writing his master's thesis on 'nothing.'" Everybody at chapel kind of stopped and said, "What?" Wendell repeated, "That's what I said. I'm talking to this guy and he says, 'I'm writing my master's thesis on nothing.' I'm not kidding ya'll."

Well, this was certainly an interesting start, different than what I expected, but Wendell had our attention.

Wendell then shared that he thought to himself at the time, "You know, I wonder, if I read that thesis would I learn anything?"

As he continued, we learned that this individual was referring to the story in the gospel of Matthew about a father whose son was suffering from convulsions caused by an evil spirit. The Bible says that these spirits tried to throw his boy into a fire and even drown him. He'd asked the apostles to deliver his son from the affliction, but they hadn't been able to heal him. There was some commotion in the crowd and Jesus came over and asked what was going on. The man shared his story and Jesus quickly stated:

> "You unbelieving and perverse generation," Jesus replied, "how long shall I stay with you? How long shall I put up with you? Bring the boy here to me." Jesus rebuked the demon, and it came out of the boy, and he was healed at that moment. (Matthew 17:17 – 18)

Afterward, probably embarrassed, the apostles privately asked Jesus why they hadn't been able to deliver the boy from the spirit. He responded, "Because you have so little faith. Truly I tell you, if you have faith as small as a mustard seed, you can say to this mountain, 'Move from here to there,' and it will move. *Nothing will be impossible for you*" (Matthew 17:20, emphasis added).

When you stop and think about it, the genesis of what Wendell was saying to all of us was that if we belong to the Lord and have faith in Christ, there's really nothing impossible for us through our Savior, Jesus Christ. It turned out to be a great chapel service, saying a lot to me and encouraging the guys.

Whom do you trust in the face of adversity? Are you like Paul in 2 Corinthians 1:8 – 10, who found himself in a situation so dire he considered it equal to having a death sentence, yet had the faith to believe in the Lord's eventual deliverance? Or maybe like Daniel, calmly trusting the Lord even unto possible death in the lions' den (Daniel 6:16 – 20)? Well, if you're like me, your first desire might just be to get out of the situation entirely. None of us truly wants to go through the tough times if we don't have to. Yet the truth is, going through these experiences can lead us to valuable learning situations.

In the Bible, the Lord lays out a few principles for us to follow in the face of a trial or discouragement. Number one, don't trust yourself to fix the problem. In Proverbs 28:26, He says to us, "Those who trust in themselves are fools." I've been foolish enough to trust myself more times than I'd like to admit, and I've shared some of the resulting failures with you within these pages.

Second, we see in Isaiah 2:22 that we aren't to put our trust in other "mere humans" either. Certainly I've written about having godly counsel and talking to others. This can help us by providing encouragement and holding us accountable. Yet, we are not to put our hope in others for the outcome.

When we get into a mess, whom are we to trust? God alone! In Psalm 130:5 and throughout the Bible we read that we are to count on the Lord and He will deliver us. He will ensure the outcome that is best for us. It may not always be the one we'd choose, but we can trust Him that it is what we need to experience to grow in our faith and develop our character.

We went on to beat the Saints that Sunday 16–10, but the chapel service led by Wendell provided me with a principle that I hopefully will never forget—there is *nothing* that my Lord can't do.

> *Dear Lord, please help me to have the faith to believe You can deliver me from any situation. Please help me learn not to trust myself or others for the outcome, but to trust You alone. Please help me to fix my eyes and hope on You, confident that there is nothing You can't do. Amen.*

TAYLOR'S LEUKEMIA

Therefore, if anyone is in Christ,
the new creation has come:
The old has gone, the new is here!
2 CORINTHIANS 5:17

My sons, J.D. and Coy, are grown men with great wives, Melissa and Heather, and each has four kids. Both families live in Charlotte, so Pat and I are really blessed to spend a lot of time with our grandchildren. As good as this may sound, our family has faced some tremendous challenges. A few years ago when J.D. and Melissa's fourth son, Taylor, was only two, he became seriously ill. The doctors feared that he might have leukemia, an aggressive cancer affecting blood and bone marrow.

The day we waited at the hospital to learn the final di-
agnosis of Taylor's disease is one I'll never forget and hope
never to experience again. We'd seen a lot of older kids
at the medical center who were suffering from what we
dreaded Taylor might have. The doctors had done their best
to prepare us for the worst, but there was nothing like seeing these children fighting this ravaging disease. It broke
your heart. What were they going through? How could their
parents bear it? Wondering whether our little Taylor might
be afflicted with the same disease was a nightmare.

We paced and prayed and consoled each other in the
waiting room. When the doctor came out to speak with us,
he confirmed our worst fear. Taylor had leukemia. We were
devastated.

Since that day, Taylor has survived intense chemo-
therapy regimens and numerous medical procedures.
He has the greatest spirit, but if there's anything that will
knock you over as a parent or grandparent, it's watching a
child fight a disease like leukemia. The surgeon put a port
into little Taylor's chest so he could receive his injections.
Periodically, Taylor would have to be put to sleep, and
he knew the regimen. As the doctors would give him his
"sleepy" medicine, as Taylor called it, I can vividly remember his "Oh, no," in a quiet child's voice. He knew what he
had to go through to fight the cancer. His struggles just
broke our hearts.

J.D. and Melissa set their minds and hearts on doing
everything possible to make Taylor's life "normal" and
to bring in the best medical care they could find for him.
Melissa created a tight network of friends and family who
encircled their family with prayer, encouragement, and
many sacrificial hours watching kids, going to ball games,

accompanying them to hospital visits — all kinds of acts of service.

At this time, I was in my fourth year of my second stretch as head coach of the Redskins. During a brief break in the 2007 season, I flew down to Charlotte to spend a little time with my family. Melissa and J.D. had put together a party for Taylor's third birthday and to honor the faithful friends who had stepped up to the plate to help them during this first traumatic year. At one point, they played a video with clips of everyone who had helped.

Watching that video featuring dozens of people helping Melissa and J.D. was personally painful. Not because of who was in it — these folks were heroes in my eyes. No. It was painful because of who was not in it — me. "Coach" had largely been away during one of the toughest years my family had ever faced. To be truthful, I wrote elsewhere that one of my biggest regrets in life was that I didn't spend enough time with my two sons during the critical years of their lives. I was concerned that I was making the same mistake again.

At the end of the '07 season, I circled up to talk with the whole family. Everyone was living in Charlotte, and I still had a year left on my contract with the Redskins. I can remember one discussion with J.D. during this time where he said, "Dad, everything you're living for is *here* in Charlotte." During my discussion with Coy, who was starting up our new motorcross team, he said, "Dad, I could sure use you." I let the team owner, Dan Snyder, know I'd be opting out of my fifth year of coaching and heading back to Charlotte at the end of the season. As much as I loved the Redskins and as good as Dan had been to me, it is a decision I have never regretted.

How about you? Are you living your life in the present with your family? Is anything coming between you and time with your kids? Maybe you're trying to perfect your golf game and spending hours on the links? At one point I became so enamored with racquetball that I spent a lot of time away from home playing in tournaments.

Take it from a guy who can be a slow learner at times: get on your knees and ask the Lord to show you what your priorities are and if they are in line with His expectations for your life.

Heavenly Father, You tell us in Your Word that today is a day the Lord has made, let us rejoice in it. Please help me to spend my time and treasure where it will have the most eternal impact. I confess to You that I have not always been a good steward of each precious day. Help me to be focused on storing up my treasures in heaven and on having a godly impact on those you have put in my life. Amen.

SOMETIMES
IT JUST KEEPS
COMING

*For I am convinced that neither death nor life,
neither angels nor demons, neither the present nor
the future, nor any powers, neither height
nor depth, nor anything else in all creation,
will be able to separate us from the love of God
that is in Christ Jesus our Lord.*
ROMANS 8:38 – 39

Our 2011 NASCAR season had been an extremely frustrating one. We were having an off year with some highs and lows. We had won five races in the Cup Series, but we had struggled with consistency and had a number of motor issues. Two of our cars had  made it to "The Chase" but didn't place as highly as we'd have liked. Our Nationwide program had won a total of eight races, but we had lost the Owner's Championship by three points.

The racing season had definitely been disappointing, but our family had also suffered through a lot of personal challenges toward the end of 2011. Pat summed up the frustration we felt one night when we were talking at home: "It just keeps coming, doesn't it," she said. I looked her right in the eyes and all I could say is, "It seems that way."

Now, as you read through this devotional, or if you've read my book *Game Plan for Life*, you know I'm not exactly a stranger to trying situations, but this was an easy top-five on my adversity list. What were my feelings at the time? My first response was, "Oh my gosh — this is overwhelming!" Next came discouragement, which some say is the devil's greatest weapon, and something I really have to fight against. Then, as it all came together, I became fearful. As is often the case, some of the visitors to our website, www .gameplanforlife.com, could relate to my situation. We have received postings where visitors were so discouraged they didn't think they could make it another day.

I wonder, are you going through adversity like this? If so, there is a silver lining to my story: even in the worst of times, I have tried to discipline myself to read the Bible daily and to lay out my concerns in prayer to the Lord. As I went through this rocky period, I can honestly tell you that God's Word seemed to come alive to me, providing insights and encouragement that lifted my spirits. I hope that by sharing a few of the things that Scripture revealed to me, you'll be blessed.

First, one verse jumped right out to me and really spoke to my heart. In John 14:27 God says, "My peace I give you." He offers a peace that the world does not give — that your heart may not be troubled or fearful. If you are going through tough times, make sure you memorize this verse. It sure was an encouragement to me.

Second, I was reminded to stay focused on Him and not on human beings. Many times other people do … what? They disappoint us. We need to stay focused on the Lord. "My thoughts are not your thoughts, neither are your ways my ways," the Lord tells us in Isaiah 55:8. It seems like every time I'm thinking about something that involves other people, I need to return my focus on God.

Third, we have to remember that God says in His Word that He loves us more than we love our own children or grandchildren. In fact, He loves us more than we love ourselves:

> For I am convinced that neither death nor life, neither angels nor demons, neither the present nor the future, nor any powers, neither height nor depth, nor anything else in all creation, will be able to separate us from the love of God that is in Christ Jesus our Lord. (Romans 8:38 – 39)

What does this tell us? That we have an all-powerful God who loves us, and if we ask Him to come into our life, there is nothing that can separate us from His love. Isn't that a great statement?

So many times when we find ourselves in the middle of adversity, we begin to feel overwhelmed and discouragement starts to take over. It is especially tough when the trials just seem to keep on coming. But if we just take a little time and connect with the God who gives us peace, who is more faithful than any human being, who loves us more than we love ourselves, He will help us make it through the worst of the storms.

> *Dear Heavenly Father, thank You for granting me a peace unlike any other. Thank You for being faithful and unfailing, unlike any human being. Thank You for loving me more than I love my family or myself. Grant me the courage to make it through this time and strengthen my faith during this troubling time. Amen.*

WISDOM FOR DEALING WITH LIFE'S CHALLENGES

If any of you lacks wisdom, you should ask God,
who gives generously to all without finding fault,
and it will be given to you.

JAMES 1:5

It was a traumatic time in my life. Our coaching staff on the St. Louis Cardinals — led by my first boss, Don Coryell — had been fired at the conclusion of the 1977 – 1978 season. The depression turned to elation when I received a phone call from John McKay with the Tampa Bay Bucs. He wanted to talk to me about becoming his offensive coordinator. I jumped on it!

But, as I told you in other pages, that season with the Bucs didn't go well. After losing the first two games, I'll never forget the post-game press conference when a reporter asked Coach McKay what he thought about his team's execution. "I think it'd be a good idea," was his sarcastic response.

He was a great coach, but he was used to calling his own plays, and soon enough he reinserted himself as the offensive play caller, reducing my role and responsibility. I was deeply frustrated. No one would want to take a guy from a losing program and make him their head coach. And to top it off, a big part of my job was gone.

As the season wound down, I began agonizing over whether to stay or try and find another coaching situation. I learned that Don Coryell had accepted an offer to coach the San Diego Chargers. I loved coaching for Don both at SDSU and in the NFL at the St. Louis Cardinals, so I prayed, "Lord, don't have him call me unless You want me to leave Tampa Bay." Guess what? He called the next morning. The problem was he wanted an assistant coach, a demotion for me. I was torn. If I went, I'd be stepping backward, but if I stayed, there was no guarantee anything would get better.

When I met with Coach McKay about my future at Tampa, he asked me to stay as offensive coordinator, but he still wanted to call the plays. I asked for some time to think about it, and we decided to meet again the next morning. It was a long night—losing my dream kept me awake. As I left for the meeting the next morning, I told Pat, "I still don't know what we should do here." Her advice was perfect. "Just let him do the talking, Joe," she said. "Say nothing until you hear all of his thoughts and plans."

When we met, he pulled out a yellow legal pad, and before I even had a chance to say anything, he started down his list of things he wanted to talk about, reiterating his desire to call the plays. The longer he talked, the more I knew it was not the right situation for me. We parted friends. I accepted the job at San Diego with Coach Coryell, but I had little peace about this decision.

I decided to hop a plane to meet with my "spiritual father," George Tharel, back in Fayetteville, Arkansas. It was snowing hard, and my connecting flight was cancelled. I was now stuck in an airport in Fort Smith, Arkansas. After collecting my bags, I overheard two guys talking about driving to Fayetteville, and without giving them a chance to say no, I said, "I am going with you." I climbed in the backseat, and we started down the snow-covered freeway. After about a mile, it dawned on me these guys were not going to make it. I informed them I wanted them to pull over and let me out. I climbed over the center divider on the freeway, bags and all, and hitchhiked right back to the airport. I was freezing and dejected and booked my flight back home.

Thawing out at the gate, my eye caught a Bible laying on a table next to my seat. Though it was a little unusual to find a Bible sitting in an airport terminal, I picked it up and began reading the first chapter of James. I'd been studying this particular chapter where it talks about godly wisdom in making decisions. Out of the blue, a guy seated next to me nudged me on the shoulder and told me that he'd recently claimed that chapter of James in his own life. "What?" I sputtered, truthfully taken aback.

This guy — a total stranger — was a pharmacist. He'd left his position to chase a dream job in another state. Upon arrival, he learned he'd have to take a tough test to be certified, though he had long since been out of school.

He'd uprooted his family, left a comfortable life, and now faced a career nightmare.

At the end of his rope, he read James for wisdom, telling the Lord, "I'm done. I'm turning this over to You. You know what I want to do in life, but I can't do this. I'm just going to have to trust You." He went ahead and took the test. "I breezed the hard test, which seemed like an impossibility at the time, and I accepted my dream job."

What I needed to do was place my career decisions in God's hands. A lot of people would say that this was just an accidental meeting, but common sense tells me that God put this person in my life at this particular time, or was he an angel God placed there to reveal his message of encouragement? I had to do my best and let God handle the rest. The only open door I had was in San Diego, and I walked through it.

Two weeks after I arrived, the offensive coordinator left for another team, and the job of helping direct the offense became mine. Two years later, after setting many offensive records with quarterback Dan Fouts and the famous Air Coryell offense, Jack Kent Cooke asked me to be the head coach of the Washington Redskins.

Are you currently facing a career decision? Have you trusted God to direct your steps? My life is a testament to placing your career in God's hands. It is the best move I ever made. No matter what He has called you to do in life, you can rely on Him to be faithful to put you in the exact right place that you need to be.

Dear Lord, thank You for holding my future in the palm of Your hands. Please help me to realize that what You want for me is far better than

*what I can imagine and that You will provide
the opportunities I need for career advancement.
Please help me to be content where I am and to
trust my future to You. Amen.*

GOD'S PRIORITY FOR YOUR CAREER

When they had done so, they caught such a large number of fish that their nets began to break.

LUKE 5:6

Because I've been blessed to win a few NFL Super Bowls and NASCAR championships and to create some enjoyable memories in professional sports, I'm often asked to give folks 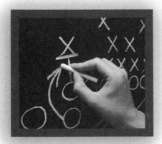 insights on career success. If you've ever heard me speak, you know I'm pretty much your "average Joe." Many of the important things I've learned in my vocation have come to me through years of competition, which include victories but also my mistakes and failures. When I've veered away from God's game plan, I have paid the price. But when I've ordered my life around God's game plan for my life, I've had some success.

In my experience, success in your vocation starts with understanding a few key principles. The first involves having the right priorities. As a Christian, you should understand that God is your first priority. Are your activities in your personal and work life reflecting this? Is your relationship with God growing? Would the people you work with know you're a Christian?

Number two on the list is your family and the influence you're having on those around you. I'm convinced that after following the Lord, this is the most important work we have to do — this will be the legacy we leave after passing from this life. The only meaningful thing we will leave on this earth will be the influence we've had on others.

Third, it is also important to involve God in your vocation. Most of us think we know what we're doing at work, but if we are honest, we spend most of our time trying to accomplish what *we* want without any consideration of what the Lord might desire. Yet if we are to keep our priorities in order, we need to be seeking what God wants, and that includes work. His involvement in our vocation ensures that we always end up with the best outcome for us — even if it is different from what we expected.

These three things seem simple enough. Yet we often get our priorities out of order. We often put career first, family a remote second, and God a distant third. Looking back on my career, having the wrong priorities invariably led me into hardship and tough times. But when my priorities were in order, I could count on the Lord to guide me through even the roughest waters.

This is why I love the story in Luke 5:1 – 11. Jesus and the disciples were on the Sea of Galilee where He was preaching the word of God to the crowd from a fishing boat. When Jesus was done teaching the crowd, He turned to Peter and said, "Put out into deep water, and let down the nets for a catch."

Peter had been fishing all night and caught nothing. So as a professional fisherman, you can just imagine him thinking, "Hey look, You may be a great teacher, but I'm the fisherman here. We've been out all night. We're the best at what we do. We have the best equipment. What did we get? The big zero. Nothing. Now You want me to go back out?"

But Peter didn't respond this way. Instead, he responded with complete obedience. "Master," he said, "we've worked hard all night and haven't caught anything. But because You say so, I will let down the nets." The disciples were faithful and rowed back out. The result? Their nets couldn't contain all of the fish they caught. They needed another boat to help bring in the catch. What this event illustrates to me is that if God is not in our efforts, it is possible to get the big ZERO; and if he is in our efforts, the results can be overwhelming.

I've had times like this in the NFL and NASCAR. In my last season with the Redskins, I remember one particularly rough patch. We'd lost three games in a row and now were about to face the best teams in the division, starting with the Giants in the Meadowlands. I honestly couldn't see the horizon or any way to turn things around. But in my prayer time and Bible reading, I had a peace to simply stay the course. It turns out that we beat the Giants and went on to win our last four games in a row, which put us in the playoffs.

How about you? Do you have your priorities in order? Are you making God first in your life and first in your career? Are you going through a tough spell? If so, what is the Lord trying to teach you? Perhaps to pray for guidance? Or to make decisions with His principles in mind rather than your own?

Thank You, Lord, for giving me the gifts for the vocation You have called me to do. Help me keep my priorities straight and to involve You in everything I do. Help me to seek You when times are good at work and when they are not so good. Help me to glorify You with the gifts You've given me. Amen.

TRUSTING
THE PLAYBOOK

Your word, LORD, is eternal;
it stands firm in the heavens.
PSALM 119:89

Imagine for a moment that you are an Arab shepherd boy in the following situation. The year is 1947, and you are looking for a lost sheep when you stumble on a cave in the lime-

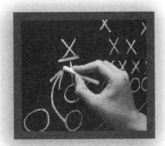

stone cliffs on the northwestern shore of the Dead Sea. Out of curiosity, you decide to throw a rock into the cave, and to your amazement, you hear the sound of breaking pottery.

You have just made the greatest manuscript discovery of modern times. These manuscripts will be known as "The Dead Sea Scrolls." Scholars date the scrolls between 250 BC and about 68 CE. These scrolls have authenticated the antiquity of many books of the Bible, such as Isaiah in the Old Testament.

The Bible is one of the most historically valid testaments in human history. Over 25,000 portions of New Testament manuscripts are available to scholars today. Great archaeological discoveries like the Dead Sea Scrolls have authenticated many books in the Old Testament. The vast majority of its writers witnessed events firsthand. In fact, there is more original evidence supporting the authenticity of the Bible than other great works of history from the likes of Aristotle and Plato (of which the authenticity is not challenged). The Bible is also the best-selling book in the world.

There is a lot more I could say about the authenticity of God's Word — it was written over a period of 1,500 years by more than forty authors from three continents in three different languages, but its message is consistent throughout. I'm confident telling people that the Bible is God's playbook for the game of life. But none of this really matters if you don't make an effort to read the Bible. Our coaching staff at Redskin Park could craft the best game plan in the world and hand every player a playbook full of wisdom for beating next week's opponent, but if a player just stuck the game plan in his locker and didn't look at it, what difference would it make come game time?

My life as an NFL coach and NASCAR team owner has been nothing if not hectic, but I've tried to discipline myself to read my Bible daily — even if just for a few minutes. In the toughest times, I've learned to count on the Bible to give me peace and clear insights to move ahead. I know it has the power to transform me. Different books in the Bible teach me different things — peace in the storm from

Psalms, wisdom for true success from Proverbs, hope for my life from the Gospels.

Have you learned to consistently turn to God's playbook as you play the game of life? Maybe you didn't realize how reliable its text is and therefore wrote the Bible off as outdated. Perhaps it intimidates you because it is big and contains names and places you're not familiar with. Whatever the reason, I challenge you to pull your Bible down from the shelf and really give it a try. Spend some time in God's Word every day. Pray beforehand that the Holy Spirit will help you understand it. Find a good devotional or reading plan to help you. You will not be disappointed. There are many tools to help you read and understand the Bible. You can find them at your Christian bookstore or online at sites like www.gameplanforlife.com.

Father, thank You for giving me the Bible as the playbook for my life — within its pages are the answers to the challenges I face. Help me to understand and come to rely on the Bible daily. I want to live my life to the fullest and to know You better. Please give me the patience and help me find the right tools to make the Bible my playbook for living and winning the most important game of all — the game of life. Amen.

ARE YOU READY?

I give them eternal life, and they shall never perish;
no one will snatch them out of my hand.
JOHN 10:28

At about 9:30 a.m. on a beautiful fall day, the pilot of a Lear jet flying out of Orlando was asked by Jacksonville air traffic control to reach a flying level of 39,000 feet. "Three nine zero bravo alpha," he responded and began his climb. Six minutes later air traffic control asked the Lear to change radio frequencies. No response. A few more minutes went by without a reply, and a nearby F-16 was asked to vector in close to the  Lear to make visual contact. Trying the radio twice, the pilot then moved in for a look. There was no visual damage to the plane, but he observed that the right cockpit window of the

Lear was opaque as if there were ice or condensation on the inside. Furthermore, he couldn't see into the cabin because the passenger windows seemed to be clouded and grey.

Two more military aircraft scrambled, trying to contact the plane. "We're not seeing anything inside ... he is not reacting, moving, or anything like that ... he should be able to have seen us by now," reported the lead pilot. Sometime thereafter, one engine of the Lear shut down. The plane spiraled to the ground from over 40,000 feet. The dramatic flight ended in a farmer's field in South Dakota, four hours and 1,800 miles after taking off from Orlando.

Five people died in that crash, and most of the country was aware that PGA golfer Payne Stewart was a passenger on that unresponsive Lear 35. The passenger I knew best was Robert Fraley. Robert was a friend and represented me when I coached the Redskins. He also represented other well-known sports figures including Bill Parcells, Dan Reeves, and Bill Cowher. He'd been one of the best high school quarterbacks in Alabama. He was recruited and played for the legendary Bear Bryant and the Crimson Tide.

Robert stayed in great physical shape, working out all of the time. We'd joke that he had the perfect life: a fantastic wife, traveling around the world with some of the great names in sports, golfing with clients like Payne Stewart. His agency was located on the top floor of a brand-new skyscraper in downtown Orlando. In the eyes of the world, Robert was at the top of his game.

But what I respected most about Robert was his deep Christian faith. Once when I was at Robert's house, I saw this quote on the wall in his workout room: "We must care for our bodies as though we were going to live forever, but we must care for our souls as if we are going to die tomorrow." He always wanted to be ready — not just by working out and staying in shape, or by being the best agent, or even by being a great husband. In spending time around Robert I found him to have a close spiritual walk with the Lord. I believe when the game of life ended for Robert on October 25, 1999, he knew that he was on the winning team. In fact, I believe that I could say the same for Payne Stewart as well as Van Arden, who worked with Robert.

The question is, "Are you ready today?" None of those guys were expecting their jet to malfunction, depriving them and the crew of the oxygen needed to sustain life. None could have imagined that their quick flight would turn into a national tragedy as that plane flew unpiloted until it ran out of fuel. The copilot was only twenty-six years old.

If you are ready, how about your kids and your spouse? There is nothing more important you can do for those you love than to make sure that they have a saving relationship with Jesus Christ.

> *Dear Father in heaven, I want to make sure that*
> *I'm prepared to be on the winning team when the*
> *game of life for me is over and the clock stops.*
> *I receive in my heart Jesus Christ as my Redeemer,*
> *the only way for a sinful person like me to ever be*
> *acceptable to a perfectly pure God. I confess that*
> *there is no other way to You, God, but through*
> *Your Son. Help me to share this truth with those*
> *You've put in my life. Amen.*

YOU CAN'T FAIL IF GOD IS IN IT

Immediately Jesus reached out his hand and caught him.
"You of little faith," he said, "why did you doubt?"
MATTHEW 14:31

I'm thankful for the Super Bowl victories and NASCAR championships I've been part of. But as you know by now, I'm most concerned about the impact I'll have on others,

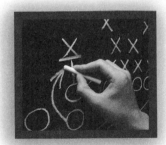

especially young people. In my first stint as Redskins head coach, I'd been trying to help at-risk teens in the D.C. area. Soon enough, it became clear that I wasn't having much impact. We needed to provide a place for these kids to live — to pull them out of their

environments and really invest in them by creating a private campus built just for them. I believe God put this project on my heart; elsewhere in this devotional I document how much of a struggle it was getting the youth home built, but we raised the funds, and I turned my focus back to winning the next Super Bowl.

As it turned out, this ministry was going to give me ample opportunities to trust the Lord. A while into the season, our accountant for the youth home called to notify me that we were $300,000 behind and in need of more operating funds. I couldn't believe it. But Gary Jones, recently hired on to help raise funds, gave me a call. He had an idea on where we could find the money. "Coach," he said, "I have a feeling we need to call the ambassador to Kuwait about this. We need to ask him to sponsor a banquet honoring the soldiers who fought the war in Kuwait." As he was telling me this, my jaw dropped, and I was thinking, "WHAT?" I gave it zero chance of success, but Gary was insistent, and I told him to go ahead and make the call.

The next day, to my amazement the ambassador wanted to meet with us. He was very nice, and after a few pleasantries he asked us why we were there to see him. Gary explained the idea. The ambassador looked at Gary and asked him how much it would cost. We told him. The ambassador said something to one of his aides, who then left the room. A few minutes later, the man returned and handed me an envelope. Inside was a check for $300,000 to sponsor the fund-raising event.

Only God could have orchestrated this miracle. In the twenty-seven years that the youth home has been operational, we have witnessed God's hand supply our needs.

Matthew 14 gives a great example of this. After feeding the five thousand on the shores of the Sea of Galilee, Jesus told the disciples to get in the boat and go on ahead.

He stayed behind to pray, and the disciples rowed the boat far off into the sea. At dawn, Jesus walked on the water to catch up with the disciples. When they saw Jesus, they were terrified, thinking He was a ghost. But Peter said, "Lord, if it is you, tell me to come to you on the water." (This is what I love about Peter — he had great courage to follow the Lord.) "Come," Jesus said, and Peter stepped out of the boat and began walking on water. But the wind picked up, and Peter was frightened and started to sink. "Lord, save me," he cried, and Jesus reached His arm across the water and rescued Peter. "You of little faith," He said, "why did you doubt?"

The Bible portrays only two individuals walking on water: Jesus and Peter. This is a great picture of having the courage to follow the Lord's calling and the humility to turn to Him when the going gets tough. Peter had the guts to step out of the boat, but like many of us, when the waves and wind kicked up, he panicked. When he called on the Lord, he was saved.

Even after many examples like the gift from the Kuwaiti ambassador, I still find myself saying, "I'll never get out of this." Maybe it's a slump in the racing season or a business situation that won't seem to change for the better. What adversity do you need to ask Jesus for help with? Maybe you have a relationship that needs repairing? Perhaps it's your job? Maybe you have a fear of financial failure? Whatever your adversity, the Lord is there for you. He wants us to have the courage to follow Him and trust Him.

Dear Heavenly Father, thank You for the many times You've blessed me by showing Your faithfulness when I've doubted. Please help me to have the courage to follow Your leading and the humility to turn to You in challenging times. I know that when You are in something, it will not fail. Amen.

STAYING STRONG UNDER CRITICISM

When all our enemies heard about this,
all the surrounding nations were afraid and
lost their self-confidence, because they realized that
this work had been done with the help of our God.
NEHEMIAH 6:16

We had just finished the 1991 pre-season with the Redskins, and to say the least, it hadn't gone well. We were 0 – 4. Even

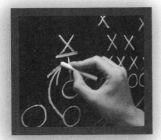

though we'd had some successful seasons in the previous few years and recently won Super Bowl XXII, the media were highly critical of our football team and coaching. As the head coach, all of that criticism landed on my front door. I've written in other pages in this book that coaching is a high-pressure occupation, and you really are only as good as your last win. Receiving strong criticism and having your abilities and decisions openly questioned is part of the job, but it is never easy. This season was getting off to a tough start, and it would only get worse for me.

I was working in my office at Redskin Park when my assistant came in. "Coach," she said, "Mr. Cooke is here, and he wants to meet with you out on the practice field." It was noon, and there were no players out on the field. I walked out to meet with Jack Kent Cooke, our team owner and my boss. Mr. Cooke was a great owner, very support-ive of me and of our coaching staff, and we had a strong relationship. One thing that always impressed me was that he was more interested in winning than making a finan-cial profit. However, it was unusual for him to want to meet with me on short notice, much less out on the practice field.

Though we always treated each other with respect, it quickly became evident that Mr. Cooke was upset. In his opinion, the team was headed toward complete disas-ter. As we continued to talk, he made a number of points. We had too many veteran players and I was too loyal to them, he explained. But Mr. Cooke really pushed my hot button when he mentioned other head coaches who he felt had taken different approaches and were prepared to take over the division, leaving the Redskins in the dust. We'd beaten a lot of these teams over the last few seasons. Mr. Cooke and I were going on our tenth year together, and this was one of the few times in our relationship when he really questioned me. I began defending our personnel de-cisions, and the discussion really became heated.

Mr. Cooke could sense how upset I was with his as-sessment. "Joe," he said, "let's go upstairs, get some coffee, and give ourselves a chance to cool off a bit."

Criticism from the press was tough enough, but to have Mr. Cooke share his doubts just as we were starting the season really stung. But I did cool off, and I did ponder what Mr. Cooke had said. I had learned over the years to respect Mr. Cooke's opinions, but after thinking through his questioning of the team, I had confidence we were headed in the right direction and it would be best to stick with the strategy we had developed for the season.

Many times as we endeavor to accomplish what we believe we are called to do, we find ourselves under criticism, whether it is the negative media or challenges coming from those we respect. It can become easy to cave in to pressures and self-doubt. But we need to stick with our convictions. Consider Nehemiah. He struggled with the rebuilding of Jerusalem's walls; his leadership was mocked, and he had great opposition to this project. But he felt God had given him this project, and his efforts resulted in one of the great victories recorded in God's Word.

Maybe you've worked really hard on a project that you know will be good for your church or business and have gone without any praise for your efforts. Perhaps you even received some criticism and doubt about your efforts. Maybe someone you highly regard is questioning your ability and judgment just when you need him or her to support you most. If so, keep the faith. As we started the 1991 season, I really had to lean on my faith in God. I made it a priority to diligently study His Word and to seek godly support from Pat and some of my friends. Doing this sustained me, helping to screen out the negatives and allowing me to focus on doing what I was called to do.

By the way, that 1991 season turned out to be pretty good. The Redskins ended up winning the first eleven games of the regular season and went on to win our third Super Bowl. ESPN later named the 1991 team the fourth greatest football team of all time.

Heavenly Father, You tell us in Your Word that we will face trials and adversity, and sometimes we experience that through the criticism of others. But You also tell us that when we persevere in trials our faith is perfected. Please help me be strong in the face of criticism and to avoid doubting and caving in to pressures I know are not of Your making. Please help me to perfect my faith, that in the end You may be glorified. Amen.

MAN OF PURPOSE

*But whatever were gains to me I now
consider loss for the sake of Christ.*
PHILIPPIANS 3:7

"Why can't we all be friends?" joked the lanky young man wearing the bright yellow fire suit as some spectators booed when it was his turn to take the microphone and introduce  himself. To a lot of folks, Kyle Busch, the driver of our #18 car, is one of NASCAR's "bad boys," and the spectators at the 160,000-seat Bristol Motor Speedway were giving him a friendly reminder of this. A fierce competitor with extraordinary talent, Kyle has a focus and passion for winning that I've rarely witnessed in my dealings with pro athletes.

The truth is that Kyle is like a magnet for action on the

track. If we've got him in a fast car, he'll be at the front of the pack battling with the fastest cars for every square inch of track. He sees opportunities and openings between cars that other drivers don't, and he goes for them. At speeds reaching 200 miles per hour, you bet that can cause some real fireworks.

Here's what a lot of people might not know about Kyle. Besides his lightning-quick reflexes and competitive nature, he also is very bright when it comes to understanding the mechanical aspects of a race car. NASCAR doesn't allow us to build technology into the car to analyze the adjustments we need to make it faster during a race. But before coming in for a pit stop, Kyle will get on the radio and let his crew chief know exactly what the car needs to do better — the same security on corner entry, more ability to turn through the center with front tire grip, and more forward drive grip with the rear tires on corner exit. He's a born racer. Even guys he's feuded with are quick to acknowledge Kyle's giftedness. Kyle is the perfect example of a man of purpose. When he's out on that track, his only purpose is to win races.

You and I need that kind of focus and purpose in the game of life. What's our purpose? We want to be on the winning team — God's team — when the clock stops ticking. To me, that means we need to experience the power of Christ's resurrection in our own lives and to share it with others: "Forgetting what is behind and straining toward what is ahead, I press on toward the goal to win the prize for which God has called me heavenward in Christ Jesus" (Philippians 3:13 – 14). Jesus is not only our salvation, but He is also the example God the Father gave us after which to model our lives.

In my own life, I accepted the fact that salvation was from Christ alone when I was a boy but did not strive to live a godly life until I rededicated my life in my early thirties. There is only one perfect human who has ever lived, and I will never be perfect like Jesus, but if I know my purpose, I will strive to follow His example. You can tell from some of the experiences I share in this book that I often fall short of the mark, but I'm committed to trying my best until the day comes for me to be with the Lord. As believers, once we are clear on our primary purpose in life, everything falls into line.

Getting back to Kyle — he won this particular race at Bristol. It was his fifth straight win at the track, a NASCAR record. ESPN labeled him "The King of Bristol." We've noticed as Kyle continues to win races, he is maturing in the way he handles all the ups and downs that surround the NASCAR circuit; at least as of the time of this writing he's getting more and more cheers and less of the "bad boy" boos. And he continues to keep his focus on the goal. What about you? Are you exhibiting the kind of focus you need to be successful in your career? If not, what changes do you need to make?

Father, help me to have the focus on my profession that can only come from You. You, Father, have blessed us with God-given talents. It is our prayer that we will use these talents to live a life of purpose for You. Amen.

TEAMMATES IN THE GAME OF LIFE

Now you are the body of Christ,
and each one of you is a part of it.
1 CORINTHIANS 12:27

The Die Hard 500 at Talladega in July 1996 stands out to me as one of the highlights of my NASCAR career. Though our performance was good — Bobby Labonte started in twenty-fourth and made his way up the field to eighth for a top-ten finish — it was not remarkable. The reason this race is etched in my memory is because our primary sponsor, Interstate Batteries, asked us to create a burgundy and gold paint scheme for the #18 car.  Rather than the usual bright green and black, the car bore the unmistakable colors of the Washington Redskins. Emblazoned on the hood was the Pro Football Hall of Fame logo. The car even had the familiar red, white, and blue NFL mark on it.

You see, the night before that race in Talladega I was inducted into the Pro Football Hall of Fame, and Interstate wanted to celebrate the occasion with the special paint job. The honor of becoming a pro football Hall of Famer and, on top of that, having a NASCAR Cup car painted to commemorate the event before thousands of racing fans was testament to God's work in my life.

As excited as I was to be inducted into the Hall of Fame, I knew this special recognition was a result of more than just my personal accomplishments. I've always believed that success in competitive sports is the result of the people you have on your team. In football, it's not about Xs and Os or trick plays; in racing it's not about technology, parts, and pieces. It's all about the talented and dedicated individuals who put the interests of the team above their own to try to achieve something great. In a *Washington Post* interview prior to the induction ceremony, I tried to convey this sentiment to the reporter:

> Gibbs said he hasn't forgotten that former Redskins general manager Bobby Beathard gave him a chance to be a head coach, or that team owner Jack Kent Cooke provided virtually endless resources as well as support through good times and bad. And there's a long list of assistant coaches and players.
>
> "The most fun in coaching was the personalities of the assistant coaches and players, all of us almost living together for six months and trying to build something," Gibbs said. "Those are the things you remember as great."[3]

At the Saturday night induction ceremony, Don Coryell — my coach at San Diego State and someone who taught
me a lot about coaching — introduced me. Don created the
unstoppable San Diego Chargers offense that was so good
at the passing game it was nicknamed "Air Coryell." Having
worked under Don, I was blessed to have a part in that success, and it was from that position that the Redskins took
notice, offering me the opportunity to be their head coach.

To go from the Pro Football Hall of Fame Saturday
night to Talladega the next day and see our car painted in
Redskins colors was humbling and reminded me of God's
graciousness. Not only had He provided opportunities and
platforms for me to reach the top levels in two competitive sports I loved, but He'd also put some amazing people
in my life along the way. In 1 Corinthians 12, the apostle
Paul writes that the body of Christ is made of many parts,
all equally important, "Even so the body is not made up of
one part but of many" (1 Corinthians 12:14). In my case, it
would be easy to name a lot of the well-known individuals
who have contributed to my career. But more important
than anyone else was my family: Pat, J.D., and Coy. They've
helped me to succeed in more areas than professional
sports.

In fact, as much as I admired Don Coryell, he was
actually my second choice to give my introduction to the
1996 Hall of Fame Class. When I was first notified that I
was chosen, my hope was to have J.D. and Coy make the
introduction for me. However, I was told I'd have to choose
just one presenter; so rather than choosing one son over
the other, I asked Don.

Whom has the Lord put around you to help you succeed in the game of life? If you are married, your spouse is

one key player on your team. If you have kids, they're next. Whether married or single, old or young, all of us have key people that we play the game of life with, and I firmly believe that our Head Coach, God, designed us to rely on and interact with others.

Dear Lord, help me to be a great teammate to those You have placed around me and help us recognize that You are our Head Coach. Help us to play the game of life in the right way so that we may have victory with You. Amen.

THE FOURTH QUARTER

Do not store up for yourselves treasures on earth,
where moths and vermin destroy, and where thieves
break in and steal. But store up for yourselves treasures
in heaven, where moths and vermin do not destroy,
and where thieves do not break in and steal.
MATTHEW 6:19 – 20

I found myself sitting in a lonely hotel room in Detroit. I was competing in a racquetball tournament over the weekend. As I lay on the bed in this lonely atmosphere, it dawned on me that Pat and my two boys were hundreds of miles away.

I must confess to you that I've struggled with pride all of my life, trying to win and prove something with my achievements. As far back as I can remember, my focus has been on competition. Whether football, racing, or other sports, I've always looked up to the guys who were putting it all on the line. And at times I believe it has hurt my relationship with those I value as the most important people in my life. Now that I'm a grandfather and have had a chance to compete at the highest levels in two professional sports, I've found myself asking some pretty tough questions: Where am I storing my treasures? What am I doing that has eternal value? Is it going to be Super Bowls and NASCAR championships? Or something else of greater importance?

At one point, I became infatuated with racquetball. So here I was, an assistant coach in the NFL, a job that already required an incredible amount of time and put a lot of pressure on my family, and I was spending my free time climbing up the amateur racquetball ranks.

What was I thinking?

Throughout this devotional I refer to the Bible as our playbook, the one perfectly crafted document to guide you and me to experience true success in the game of life. If there is one theme that runs throughout the Bible — from the fall of Adam and Eve in the first pages of Genesis to the second coming of Christ in Revelation — it is redemption. I believe that when we acknowledge our shortcomings and confess our sins, our Lord will often help us to redeem the situations in which we find ourselves in life. In this instance, when it became clear to me that my priorities were out of order, I needed to ask for forgiveness from the Lord and from the people who had been impacted by my choices — my family.

I'm thankful to have great relationships with Pat, J.D., and Coy, but a few years ago I took each of the boys to lunch specifically to apologize to them. I should have found a way to spend more time with them. I let them know it was one of the single biggest mistakes of my life. Though I could not make up the time I lost with them as boys, I would try to do so with them as adults. I wouldn't make the same mistake with my grandkids either. This is one place, maybe the most important, where I should be storing up treasures that will have eternal consequences.

What is it for you? Maybe it's your job, your golf game, or acquiring money. What do you truly treasure? Even if you are like me and in the fourth quarter of life, you can be storing up treasures with eternal outcomes. If you have a family, there is nothing better you can do than to spend time shaping the values and beliefs of your kids and loving your spouse. Take the time to ask yourself if what you treasure is eternal or not. Learn from my mistake. You don't want to be wishing you could have done things differently when the clock on your life runs out.

Lord, help me see what is of eternal value in my life. Help me to see where I am merely storing up treasures that can be destroyed and help me to give those treasures up for ones that have eternal value. I know that in Your strength I can make the changes I need to make to finish strong. Amen.

REFUSING TO LOSE

*May the Lord direct your hearts into God's love
and Christ's perseverance.*
2 THESSALONIANS 3:5

In the midst of sleet and snow, I called a timeout with just 2:10 left in the half. As we huddled on the sideline, our

quarterback, Joe Theismann, looked pretty beat up. He'd been sacked hard and had already thrown three interceptions; the number on his jersey was hard to read. Joe had spent a lot of time on the ground. His two front teeth were broken in half, and he was spitting blood. I was thinking to myself that this might be the time Joe told me, "I think I might take the rest of the half off." But after looking him in the eyes, I knew his focus was on one thing: beating the Giants and securing a spot in the NFL playoffs. Everything else was secondary — his broken teeth, the sacks, the weather.

The second half was no piece of cake. We started down by eleven points. As the weather got steadily worse, the game would be decided in the final drive from our 29-yard line with 3:28 left. We had whittled the Giants' lead to two points, and Joe orchestrated a final drive that led to a Mark Moseley 39-yard field goal, giving us a 15 – 14 victory with four seconds to spare.

Asked about his four interceptions prior to the final drive, Joe said, "I made a mistake on each one, and I knew what it was, so there was no reason to lose confidence." He didn't worry about past mistakes or future obstacles; his purpose was to win that game. To this day, his resolve on that snowy day sticks in my mind when asked what kind of player Joe "T" was. Joe knew what his purpose was that day — to lead his team to victory — and that was his only focus.

When it comes to living a life of purpose, it can be easy for us to lose focus, especially in the face of adversity and challenges. In 2 Corinthians 5, we learn that we are new creations in Christ (2 Corinthians 5:17), reconciled to a Holy God through Jesus. Because of this, we are "Christ's ambassadors, as though God were making his appeal" to others through us. That is our purpose — to be a new creation in Christ and to share His love with others. We can't worry about mistakes we've made in the past, and we can't duck our responsibility in the face of adversity. I like this story about Joe Thiesmann because he didn't focus on his mistakes and he didn't take the easy way out when he could have done that. It is a model of perseverance.

Living the Christian life and being an ambassador for Christ is not easy for anyone, including me. Hey, I'll be honest, a lot of guys don't agree with me. In fact, they may respect me for what I've accomplished in the NFL or in NASCAR but have a big question mark in their minds when it comes to my beliefs; they're not sure about God or the Bible. I understand this, and it doesn't bother me. It would be my hope that by sharing what God has done in my life, I can be a witness that may help point them toward Christ.

Because the Christian walk takes perseverance, some folks try to go halfway. They acknowledge their need for a Savior, accept Christ into their lives, but don't play the game of life with a sense of purpose. I did this until rededicating my life at age thirty-two. Prior to that, I was a "new creation" in Christ, but I was not living for Him. But the Lord used George Tharel, and some others whom God placed in my life, to show me how to live for Christ. George was living out his life on purpose by being a devoted Sunday school teacher.

Going back to that freezing game at RFK Stadium, whenever I think of it, I remember a guy who would not come off the field until his purpose was accomplished. That is the kind of resolve you and I need to have every day to accomplish what God has called us to do on this earth.

Heavenly Father, I want to be a man of purpose doing what You've created me to accomplish during this lifetime. Please help me stay focused on Your purposes for my life and to avoid distractions. I pray that You will help me stay on course so that at the end of my life, I can with all humility be counted as a faithful ambassador for You. Amen.

FINDING TRUE PEACE AT NIGHT

Yes, my soul, find rest in God;
my hope comes from him.
PSALM 62:5

Have you ever been dead tired and gone to bed only to find yourself too anxious to fall asleep? It happens to me more than I care to admit — the quieter the night gets, the more my mind races. One night recently,  all I could think about was the board meeting one of our primary sponsors would be having the next morning; they'd be considering whether to extend the company's ongoing relationship with Joe Gibbs Racing. The decision would have a huge impact on our racing program.

As I lay there tossing and turning, trying not to wake up Pat, all of the questions and concerns I could think about rolled around in my head. Had we done everything we needed to do? Did I talk to the executives I needed to talk to? How about the leadership at the race shop — had we missed anything important? Then, of course, I started thinking about how bad the economy was — many Fortune 500 companies like our sponsor were analyzing every dollar spent.

No matter what your circumstances, there's always something in your life you can't control that will keep you up at night. But trials are a part of life. The apostle James writes, "Consider it pure joy, my brothers and sisters, whenever you face trials of many kinds, because you know that the testing of your faith produces perseverance" (James 1:2 – 3). James does not write "if" we face trials; he writes "whenever" we face them.

Since we will face trials, it is important to keep them in perspective. A devotional book I read often in my quiet time[4] has some great insights that I hope can help you as much as they helped me. It describes four principles to practice when dealing with anxiety.

First, don't worry about the situation. All that does is keep you from resting. Instead, take your concerns and prayerfully put them before the Lord: "Do not be anxious about anything, but in every situation, by prayer and petition, with thanksgiving, present your requests to God" (Philippians 4:6).

Second, don't try and figure it out. Instead, look to God who has already figured it out. "For my thoughts are not your thoughts," we read in Isaiah 55:8. The Lord is the Creator of the universe and knows everything that has happened and will happen. He knows how your situation will end up already, and however it does, it will be best for you.

The third principle is particularly tough for me: don't try and make something happen. Many of the circumstances that cause us anxiety are ultimately not in our control. I lay there that night worrying about our sponsor's board meeting the next day, but the truth was that we'd done everything we could do. As much as I may have wanted to kick in the door and make something happen, there was nothing left to do. Repeatedly in the Bible we are told: "Blessed are all who wait for [the LORD]" (Isaiah 30:18).

Lastly, we've got to commit ourselves to trust God for the outcome of the situation. Proverbs 3:5–6 says, "Trust in the LORD with all your heart and lean not on your own understanding; in all your ways submit to him, and he will make your paths straight." I've had many situations turn out much differently than I thought they would. But as I hope you can tell from the pages of this book, I've learned through these situations perhaps nothing is more important than to trust the Lord.

As it turns out, our sponsor extended their agreement with the race team, and we continue to be great partners. My anxiety that night didn't change anything, it just made me a little tired the next day!

Dear Lord, please help me find peace in the night that only You can provide. Help me to wait on You, to trust You, and to be content in You. Help me to continually give all that I do back to You, trusting You for the outcome that is best for me in every situation. Amen.

A GRANDSON'S LOVE

For the eyes of the LORD range throughout
the earth to strengthen those whose hearts
are fully committed to him.

2 CHRONICLES 16:9

Coaching in the pros is so demanding that it requires most of your waking time during the season — and in the off-season as well. During my second stint with the Redskins I had a twelve-hour break during a busy pre-season week, and I used it to slip off from Redskin Park to our beach house in South Carolina. I was looking forward to spending some time watching the grandkids play on the beach.

Man, twelve hours can sure go by fast! I spent the last hour of my short stay sitting in a beach chair watching our grandkids enjoy playtime on the beach. Then, with it already time to head back to Washington, I said my good-byes to everyone. Jackson, my oldest grandson, who was about ten years old at the time, said, "Coach, I want to ride back to the airport with you."

"Nah, Jackson," I told him, "Don't do that. Stay here and play because you guys are having so much fun. You'll waste a couple of hours." But he insisted, so Jackson, Grandma, and Coach headed to the airport.

Knowing that it would be a few weeks before I had another break and would be able to catch up with them, I enjoyed visiting with Jackson and Pat during our thirty-minute ride. We said our good-byes and I headed for the airplane, leaving Jackson and Grandma standing on the tarmac watching our plane taxi down the runway.

That night, talking to Pat on the phone, she told me that when I'd climbed into the plane to fly off, she'd asked Jackson if he was ready to leave the airport.

"No, Grandma."

Each time she suggested they leave for the car, Jackson replied, "No, I want to watch Coach leave."

Pat assured me that even though he couldn't really see me in the plane, Jackson stayed until I was out of sight.

I pray about my relationship with my grandkids, and I can't tell you how much pleasure I have experienced with all eight of them. Jackson's love for "Coach" was evident, and when Pat told me of his desire to stay and see me off, I got emotional just thinking about it. This little guy didn't know if I could see him or not, but he was not leaving that airport until he couldn't see me any longer.

This experience led me to think about our relationship with our Lord. We are His children, and just like Jackson intently watching me in the airplane without actually seeing me, we can't see our Heavenly Father. But He is there for us. Jackson's love was demonstrated by sacrificing two hours away from playtime with his brothers and cousins to see me off on this trip back to D.C. Compare that to our own lives, and it is encouraging to realize that we have an all-powerful, all-knowing, and all-loving God looking out through a window in heaven watching us. We can't see Him, but He sees you and me.

As I have watched my grandkids grow, my wish for them is a successful and joyful life. Studying God's Word, we realize that as He looks down on us, He has promised us a successful life when we seek His guidance and direction. It's encouraging for me to know that God loves me even more than I love Jackson and that He is always looking out for those who love Him: "For the eyes of the LORD range throughout the earth to strengthen those whose hearts are fully committed to him" (2 Chronicles 16:9). The context here is a battle, but the message is that when we are committed to trusting the Lord, His heart is to seek us out and to give us strength. He never quits on us. In fact, God loves us even more than we love ourselves and always wants what is best for us.

Do you have peace inside knowing that Your Heavenly Father is always watching you and wants the best for you even when you can't see Him? Do you have that joy in your life that reflects the love your Heavenly Father has for you? Are you living your life for Him?

Father, please help me remember that Your eyes are always seeking me with a love that is greater than any I will ever know on earth. Please help me live in the joy and peace of this realization. Amen.

NOTHING IS IMPOSSIBLE FOR GOD

This is an easy thing in the eyes of the LORD.
2 KINGS 3:18

"Do you want it?" the official asked. Caught up in the emotions, I responded, "Yes." With that came the biggest mistake of my coaching career. We were up 16–14 over the Buffalo Bills with about a minute left in the game. Now they could

win with a field goal. The weather conditions were going to make it tough for a 51-yard field goal, but I still wanted to ice the kicker. There was a lot of emotion in this game. Sean Taylor's life had been taken a week earlier and our team had played its heart out.

I called a timeout to ice the kicker. My mistake was that I called a second timeout, and the rules of the NFL state you cannot call two timeouts in a row without running a play in between. We were penalized fifteen yards. It put the Bills' kicker in better range, and he made the kick. We lost 17 – 16. I had let my guys down after one of the worst weeks in the history of the Redskins.

Leaving FedEx Field, I was as low as I'd ever been in my entire career. Questioning my judgment and leadership, I went into a tailspin. The press would be asking if the game had passed me by. The team would have their confidence in me shaken. But the Chicago Bears were coming into town on Thursday, so I didn't have time to dwell on my mistake. I had to regain my composure and focus on the Bears. This is where the Bible became real for me.

Reading 2 Kings 3 in my Bible study during this time, I studied the story of Jehoshaphat. Marching through a desert to battle, his army had run out of water. Looking for guidance, Jehoshaphat sought out the prophet Elisha and asked him what God said about the situation. Elisha told him, "This is what the LORD says: Make this valley full of ditches. For this is what the LORD says: You will see neither wind nor rain, yet this valley will be filled with water, and you, your cattle and your other animals will drink. This is an easy thing in the eyes of the LORD; he will also hand Moab over to you" (2 Kings 3:16 – 18, NIV 1984).

I found myself putting me in the place of Jehoshaphat. I was going to be telling men to start digging ditches in this valley. I could imagine what his army thought. These verses really spoke to me. Not only was God going to provide for Jehoshaphat's army; it was an *easy* thing for him to do. The next morning the valley was overflowing with water.

Like Jehoshaphat who could see neither wind nor rain, I couldn't see any relief for the team or for myself. But also like Jehoshaphat, I needed to be faithful and put my focus on the remaining games in the season. Getting through this trial would be an easy thing in the eyes of the Lord. My job? Be faithful and plow ahead the best I could. This story from a 2,500-year-old book gave me the peace and hope I needed to concentrate, and it helped me to focus on the remainder of the season and leave the outcome up to God. We went on to the playoffs after winning the next four games against some of the toughest NFC teams — the Bears, Vikings, Giants, and Cowboys.

Have you made some big mistakes in your life or found yourself in a situation that looks as if there is no hope? You may find yourself parallel to Jehoshaphat's situation. I think we need to remember the answer can be *easy in the eyes of the Lord*.

> *Heavenly Father, please help me to look to You in my times of need. Where I don't see any provision, You provide. Where I don't see any hope, it is an easy thing for You. Help me to keep my eyes fixed on You and Your promises, not on the obstacles I face. Amen.*

IT COULD END
AT ANY TIME

"He will wipe every tear from their eyes.
There will be no more death" or mourning or crying or pain,
for the old order of things has passed away.
REVELATION 21:4

My heart stopped momentarily as I watched our #20 car flying through the air, eventually landing on our #18 car. These guys had been racing at speeds close to 200 miles per hour at Daytona International Speed-way. A ton-and-a-half of the most so-phisticated racing technology in the world seemed to defy gravity, doing something it was never designed to do. When our cars finally tumbled to a stop in the infield, time went into slow motion as we waited for a response from the drivers. Tony Stewart and Bobby Labonte both dropped their window nets, a sign to the safety crew that they were okay.

The accident on lap 173, later called the "Big One" by the media, involved eighteen cars and ended the day for our teams. It was definitely a disappointing way to end the race, but at least our two drivers hadn't been hurt despite the heart-stopping accident they'd survived. Yet, however bad that wreck seemed, this particular race would forever be remembered for something far worse.

Twenty-two laps later, with only one lap remaining in the race, Dale Earnhardt's famed #3 GM Goodwrench car hit the retaining wall. As a choked-up Mike Helton, president of NASCAR, later explained to the press, "After the accident in turn four at the end of the Daytona 500, we've lost Dale Earnhardt." I was at the local hospital with Tony Stewart making sure he was okay when I got the word of the fatal crash. Dale Earnhardt was only forty-nine years old. There was a half-mile left in the 500-mile race. Now we had lost the most iconic driver in our sport, a guy so competitive he was appropriately nicknamed "The Intimidator." Just like that, a living legend and arguably the most important figure in modern NASCAR history was gone. Most of us were stunned.

The Bible tells us that our life is like the grass that withers in the field, and it is over before we know it (Psalm 103:15). God's Word also tells us that we have souls that will live eternally (John 3:15 – 16). You might expect that NASCAR drivers would be used to facing death — after all they're racing around speedways like Daytona at 200 miles per hour. To some degree, drivers are more accustomed to higher risks. Yet in my experience, most people really don't think all that much about eternity. Most of us really aren't prepared for life to end.

As a Christian, I know that my eternal salvation is assured. Yet for a long time, I punted when it came to thinking about Heaven. It used to be a vague notion to me, not as compelling as my "real" life. But as a coach and team owner competing in professional sports, I knew our teams needed an objective to focus on to win. For you and me, I believe we need to focus on winning the game of life. That means being able to look up at the scoreboard at the end of the game and see our names on the winning team's side. It means we will be going to Heaven.

Jesus is preparing a place in Heaven for those who believe in Him and understand that He is the only way that we can get there (John 14:1 – 4). Heaven is where all of the pains of this life will disappear (Revelation 21:4). It is going to be the new earth, and the old earth will be forgotten (Isaiah 65:17). I've spent a lot of time understanding Heaven from reading Randy Alcorn's book titled *Heaven* and his chapter in *Game Plan for Life,* which helped me gain a more in-depth understanding of Heaven. I'm actually excited that I'll be there one day. After all, Jesus is making a room in His Father's house just for me. Can anything be better than what He could prepare for me?

Sometimes it takes a tragedy to grab our attention. Maybe it is something close to home — the passing of an acquaintance or family member. Maybe it is something as shocking as losing a larger-than-life icon like Dale Earnhardt, who truly seemed invincible. One day we will not be on this earth. Are you ready? Do you have an eternal view of your life? Do you have a clear picture of Heaven and understand how you can get there?

Dear Lord, I know that one day I will no longer reside on earth. But I also know that my soul will live forever. Your Word tells me that You have a mansion with many rooms and that Jesus is preparing a room for me. Help me to understand that Heaven is a real place and being there with You throughout eternity should be my goal. Help me become excited about Heaven. Amen.

AUDIENCE OF ONE

His master replied, "Well done, good and faithful servant!
You have been faithful with a few things;
I will put you in charge of many things.
Come and share your master's happiness!"
MATTHEW 25:23

If you are reading this book, my guess is that you hope to one day stand before the Lord and hear Him utter this great compliment: "Well done, good and faithful servant." If this is true for you, one of the most important lessons you can learn is to know who you are working for.

We all tend to play to the audience that we believe is most vital to our success and well-being. If you're a football player, your audience might be your coach or your teammates. A top

NASCAR driver has his sponsors, fans, and race team he thinks about satisfying. The funny thing is that ultimately — as Os Guinness wrote in his chapter on vocation in my book *Game Plan for Life*[5] — every one of us is playing to an even more important audience than we often realize or remember. It is an audience of one: God. Yes, players need fans, writers need readers, and leaders need followers. These are their worldly audiences. But ultimately, it is what God thinks that matters most to any of us playing the game of life. In my life, I've found this to be a particularly valuable principle to keep in mind, especially when it comes to my career.

You've probably picked up by now that I've learned the most in my life when facing adversity, especially as it relates to work. I've labored through losing streaks with literally no hope that anything will turn out differently, close calls in races where our driver looked like a sure winner but cut a tire and wound up in the back of the pack, and mediocre seasons that never seemed to end. Through it all, one of the most important lessons I've learned is that I can't control all of the situations I come into, but I can make sure I play to the most important audience of all: my Lord.

This reminds me about a situation last year when we thought we had a racing victory cinched only to have it snatched away by an intentional bump from a competitor in the last five laps of the race. In that case, we not only lost the race — dashing the expectations of our fans, sponsors, and driver — but to add insult to injury, one of our really fast cars was totaled. Believe me, it took all the discipline I had to control my temper.

Sometimes — like that '07 Redskins season where I drew the penalty in the last seconds of the game that may have caused us to lose to the Buffalo Bills — the Holy Spirit taught me that I was wrongly playing for a different audience of one — me! Other times, early in my career, I learned to stick to what I knew best — coaching and competition — rather than finances and real estate development. In racing, I've learned that even a mountain of adversity can be overcome by a lot of hard work and having the right people around you.

My friend Norm Miller, who runs Interstate Batteries, loves to remind me that he and I are "playing in the fourth quarter on house money" — that is to say, we've both been working for almost fifty years and are closer to the end of our careers than the beginning. To me, what ultimately matters is doing my best to please God. "Live as children of light," the apostle Paul writes in Ephesians 5, "and find out what pleases the Lord."

Where are you when it comes to pleasing the audience of one? Are you working for yourself to build riches and fame? Maybe, like me, you've actually thought at times you were doing something to please the Lord, only to realize you had other motives? If so, it's time to make sure your vocation is dedicated to the most significant audience of all, so when you stand before the Lord, you can hear those cherished words: "Well done, good and faithful servant."

Dear Lord, it sure seems like You teach us a lot through our vocations. Please help me to make sure that my performance is targeting You, the audience of one. Please show me where I'm working for other audiences — my colleagues, friends, even my family or myself — and help me focus on You and Your calling for me. Help me to glorify You through everything that I do. Amen.

STILL BATTLING

However, I consider my life worth nothing to me;
my only aim is to finish the race and complete the task
the Lord Jesus has given me — the task of testifying
to the good news of God's grace.
ACTS 20:24

Pat and I have partnered together through forty-five years of marriage. We have two grown sons with great wives and

eight grandkids. Although my family is of the utmost importance to me, I've sometimes missed the mark as a dad and husband. And as a family we have faced the most severe trials imaginable, from medical trauma Pat overcame in our earlier years to the leukemia our grandson Taylor still battles today. In my desire to create financial stability in the volatile world of coaching, I brought my family to the brink of financial ruin and created yet another crisis to overcome.

For the last four-plus decades, coaching and competing in professional sports has occupied my days. Though I've been fortunate being part of some memorable moments on the gridiron and racetrack, I've also experienced struggles in my career. I've documented some of the high points and challenges I've faced in my personal and professional life in these pages along with the lessons God has taught me along the way.

My hope is that some of the insights I've learned over the years might be helpful to you. By writing this devotional am I implying that my walk with the Lord is perfect? Hardly. Going into my seventies, I'm still learning, still a work in progress. You could definitely say I'm a life learner. "Joe" is a great name for me. Why, you might ask? Because in reality, I am your "average Joe." Maybe you can relate to that?

So, as an "average Joe," what has the Lord taught me through all of these experiences? A lot. But most significant, when I follow God's game plan for my life, I experience success. When I don't, I get hammered. It's pretty simple. As a coach I can tell you for a fact that human nature does not change and our tendency is to repeatedly make the same mistakes. Though scholars might like to say otherwise, apart from a life-change in Christ, humanity is not on a path to perfection. It is the same now as it was 1,500 years ago. The Bible is clear about this. Paul wrote in Romans, "There is no one righteous, not even one" (Romans 3:10). We tend to be prideful, self-centered, and looking for success in the eyes of the world. It really doesn't take much for us to focus on the wrong things and to mix up our priorities. In no time at all, we're following the world's game plan for our lives.

For me, in the heat of competition I might believe that I'm playing to an audience of 80,000 at FedEx Field or to 150,000 fans at the Bristol Motor Speedway. But when I take the time to pray and read my Bible, I'm reminded that I really just play for an audience of ONE — the God who created me and loves me. If He is my primary audience, everything else will fall into line — professionally and personally. Most important, I'll continue to grow spiritually.

How about you? Are you too focused on climbing the corporate ladder? Is ambition your god? Are you envious of others in your desire to look good in the eyes of the world?

Now that you've nearly finished reading this devotional and have had a chance to share in some of my failings, shortcomings, and, yes, victories, I hope you take away this one central point: there is nothing in life more important than being on God's team. His team has already won and leads to an eternity in Heaven. If you aren't sure, God has made it so simple that all you have to do is accept His Son, Jesus Christ, as Your Lord and Savior. If you'd like to do this right now, pray this prayer:

> *Lord, I recognize that You have created me, and I confess that I am a sinner. I know that You sent Your only Son, Jesus Christ, to die on the cross for my sins. I want You to come into my life and forgive me of my sins, and I want You to be my Lord and Savior.*

Take the time to find a Bible-believing church to participate in and grow spiritually from. If you've already said this prayer at some point in your life, share it with others. It is the most important legacy you can leave behind.

Father, I want to be on Your team and experience eternal life with You when the game of life ends for me here on this earth. Help me to stay focused on Your priorities for my life. Please lead me to a closer walk with You, one that will win others to Christ and serve as a testimony to the greatness of You in my life. Amen.

NOTES

1. A. W. Tozer, *The Knowledge of the Holy* (New York: Harper & Row, 1961).
2. *Racing News Daily*, February 14, 2011, "Dale Jarrett, Joe Gibbs, and Interstate Batteries Win Together, Celebrate Separately" (available at http://network.yardbarker.com/). The racing event took place at the Daytona 500 in 1993.
3. Richard Justice, "Gibbs, a Last Testament to Greatness," *Washington Post* (July 27, 1996); available at www.washingtonpost.com/wp-srv/sports/redskins/history/gibbs/articles/gibbs27.htm.
4. J. M. Farro, *Life on Purpose Devotional for Men* (Tulsa, OK: Harrison House, 2004).
5. Joe Gibbs, *Game Plan for Life: Your Personal Playbook for Success* (Carol Stream, IL: Tyndale House, 2011).